Forum 2012

The Rule of Law and the Challenges to Jurisprudence

Central and Eastern European Forum for Legal, Political, and Social Theory Yearbook

Edited by Jürgen Busch / Péter Cserne / Michael Hein / Miklós Könczöl / Miodrag Jovanović / Marta Soniewicka

Volume 3

PL ACADEMIC RESEARCH

Péter Cserne/Miklós Könczöl/Marta Soniewicka (eds.)

The Rule of Law and the Challenges to Jurisprudence

Selected papers presented at the Fourth Central and Eastern European Forum for Legal, Political and Social Theorists, Celje, 23–24 March 2012

PL ACADEMIC RESEARCH

Bibliographic Information published by the Deutsche Nationalbibliothek
The Deutsche Nationalbibliothek lists this publication
in the Deutsche Nationalbibliografie; detailed bibliographic
data is available in the internet at http://dnb.d-nb.de.

Library of Congress Cataloging-in-Publication Data
Central and Eastern European Forum for Legal, Political and Social Theorists
(4th : 2012 : Celje, Slovenia)
The rule of law and the challenges to jurisprudence : selected papers presented at the
Fourth Central and Eastern European Forum for Legal, Political and Social Theorists,
Celje, 23-24 March 2012 / Péter Cserne, Miklós Könczöl, Marta Soniewicka (eds.):
pages cm. — (Central and Eastern European Forum for Legal, Political and Social
Theory yearbook ; volume 3)
ISBN 978-3-631-64381-5
1. Rule of law—Europe, Eastern—Congresses. 2. Judicial review—Europe, Eastern—
Congresses. I. Cserne, Péter, editor of compilation. II. Soniewicka, Marta, editor of
compilation. III. Könczöl, Miklós, editor of compilation. IV. Title.
KJC4426.A6C46 2012
340'.11—dc23

2013046299

ISSN 2191-8317
ISBN 978-3-631-64381-5 (Print)
E-ISBN 978-3-653-03617-6 (E-Book)
DOI 10.3726/978-3-653-03617-6

PL Academic Research is an Imprint of Peter Lang GmbH.

Peter Lang – Frankfurt am Main · Bern · Bruxelles · New York ·
Oxford · Warszawa · Wien

This book is part of an editor's series of PL Academic Research
and was peer reviewed prior to publication.

www.peterlang.com

Contents

Contributors

Luka Burazin assistant professor, University of Zagreb, Croatia

Goran Dajović assistant professor, University of Belgrade, Serbia

Krzysztof J. Kaleta assistant professor, University of Warsaw, Poland

Ágnes Kovács PhD student, University of Debrecen, Hungary

Mojca M. Plesničar researcher, Institute of Criminology, University of Ljubljana, Slovenia

Verena Risse PhD student, Johann Wolfgang Goethe University, Frankfurt am Main, Germany

Lidia Rodak lecturer, University of Silesia, Katowice, Poland

Tilen Štajnpihler assistant lecturer, University of Ljubljana, Slovenia

Szilárd Tattay assistant professor, Pázmány Péter Catholic University, Budapest, Hungary

Sabina Zgaga assistant professor, University of Maribor, Slovenia

Editors

Péter Cserne senior lecturer, Hull University, UK

Miklós Könczöl assistant lecturer and librarian, Pázmány Péter Catholic University, Budapest, Hungary; PhD student, Durham University, UK

Marta Soniewicka assistant professor, Jagiellonian University, Kraków, Poland

Introduction

This volume is the third in the series of the Central and Eastern European Forum for Legal and Social Theory Yearbooks.

The Forum is an initiative for the cooperation and exchange of ideas among young Central and Eastern European scholars working in the field of legal, political and social theory. It has grown out of a conference held in 2009 in Katowice, Poland, where some of the participants have come to realise that the meeting filled a real gap. The next step was to make the meetings regular and the Forum at least minimally institutionalised.

Establishing the Forum was a response to the dominance of Western European and American scholarship in the field: not so much an attempt to build up a counter-power but to reflect on our problems and to articulate our views in a distinct voice. At the same time, it was also an endeavour to connect those new cohorts of academics whose career started at or after the turn of the millennium. The idea to form a group with a regional and generational character was further stimulated by the need to build a network of researchers who often live in close proximity without knowing of each other's work. Being part of a diverse and respectful scholarly community where intellectual freedom and honesty reign over hierarchy and cynicism is an experience that is regrettably uncommon in today's academia – and it is what the Forum strives to facilitate.

Apart from a vigorous online presence (www.cee-forum.org), the key activity of the Forum is to organise annual conferences that give an opportunity for junior scholars coming from or conducting research on this region of Europe to present their work before an international audience of peers. After Katowice, the conferences have taken place in Budapest, Belgrade, Celje, and Greifswald, each followed by the publication of select papers presented at the Forum.

The ten papers in this volume, selected by the Forum Board and edited by three of its members, were presented and discussed on the 23rd and 24th of March 2012 at the 4th Forum in the beautiful historic town of Celje in Slovenia. The conference provided a platform for a lively and academically rigorous debate on matters that are just too important to be left to politicians. The main topic was 'Reconsidering Democracy: (New) Theories, Policies and Social Practices', thus putting a special emphasis on recent controversies around democracy. The discussion also covered other key issues in legal, political and social theory relevant in this region or more broadly. As reflected in this volume, many of them have been concerned with the meaning and implications of the rule of law. The 4th Forum was convened by Dr. Andraž Teršek from the University of Primorska, and hosted by the International School for Social and Business Studies, with the local organisation in the able hands of Marko Smrkolj. We would like to thank them for their enthusiasm and hard work.

The generation for which, at least in most countries of the region, the pre-1989 authoritarian heritage belongs to the past and the term 'Europe' appears as a symbol of powerful political and legal ideals, had more than enough opportunity over the last two decades to realise that neither democracy nor the rule of law can be taken for granted. It seems that when it comes to these two concepts, the unease of many Central and Eastern Europeans is not simply due to a mismatch between ideals and reality or theory and practice. Rather, the malaise stems from a realisation that in spite of many advantages we enjoy simply by virtue of having grown up around or after 1989, this is no time to sit back. If we as scholars and citizens want to think and speak clearly about or effectively take a stand for our political and legal ideals, we need to reflect on them constantly, and conceptualise them in novel ways, by questioning entrenched lines of argument, reformulating old concepts and categories, and problematising established patterns of thought.

In one way or another, the contributors to this volume can be seen as doing exactly this. They raise questions and suggest new ideas on 'The Rule of Law and the Challenges for Jurisprudence', each on his or her own voice and from his or her own perspective. The contributors discuss a wide range of subjects from jurisprudential methodology and legal reasoning through democracy and constitutional courts to rights and criminal justice. One of our tasks as editors has been to arrange the papers in a meaningful order. They are divided into five thematic parts but we expect and invite readers to discover other threads that link papers throughout the book across the five parts. A short overview of the papers may prove helpful in this.

The first part comprises two papers that illuminate current problems by revisiting insights from classical jurisprudential thought. In his paper, 'The Relationship of Natural Law and Natural Rights: Organic, Contingent, or Logically Contradictory?', Szilárd Tattay argues that while the idea of natural rights is not necessary for a coherent theory of natural law, it is, *pace* Strauss and Villey, perfectly compatible with it. Inspired by the historical studies of Tierney and Brett, Tattay reconstructs how the idea of permissive natural law allowed late Scholastic thinkers to accommodate rights in natural law theory. In this way, the history of legal and political thought suggests a convincing theoretical framework for conceiving of natural law and natural rights as complementary, while maintaining continuity with the classical tradition of legal theory. Verena Risse's paper, entitled 'International Coercion and the Requirement of an International Rule of Law', turns to Kant's legal theory for answering a fundamental normative question about the international relations of our days: the validity of the principle of rule of law beyond national borders. By focusing on the Kantian understanding of the relationship between right and coercion, Risse argues that the rule of law is not tied to any specific political order. In fact, whether we consider its formal or material aspect, the conceptual structure of the principle shows that it equally concerns nation states, international organisations and the entire international domain.

The two papers in the second section contribute to current meta-theoretical and methodological debates in analytical jurisprudence. Goran Dajović's paper on 'The Subject Matter of Jurisprudence' argues that any theoretical enquiry on the nature of law should take 'folk concepts' and correlative understandings of the law as the starting point in demarcating law as a phenomenon. Conceiving of law as a social and cultural artefact, jurisprudence should then strive for the theoretical concept of law which best captures the necessary features of law as a phenomenon. The author suggests that this theoretical concept of law can diverge from and improve upon the folk concept. Luka Burazin's paper, 'Is "Naturalised" Methodology in Legal Theory Helpful?', takes up a concern about conceptual analysis also mentioned in Dajović's paper: should the *a priori* method of mainstream conceptual analysis be replaced or complemented by *a posteriori* analysis conducted empirically? The paper critically analyses Brian Leiter's proposal for the naturalisation of jurisprudence as the best known representative of this idea in today's English-speaking jurisprudence. Burazin argues that while a strong version of naturalism is misguided, Leiter's actual proposal only amounts to a combination of modest conceptual analysis and a modest version of naturalism (the latter being engaged with empirical research on the intuitions of norm addressees). In this and related limited tasks, empirical research usefully complements conceptual analysis in jurisprudence.

The third part consists of a single paper by Lidia Rodak on 'Objectivity as Coherence in Practical Discourse'. At a methodological level, the paper addresses the issue whether and how the concept of objectivity in law can be grasped in a bottom-up manner, i.e. by analysing how courts and other legal actors use the term in describing their own activity. Taking Polish and European case law as examples, she looks at the various ways objectivity is referred to in practical legal discourse. The main substantive finding of the paper is that the concept of objectivity serves as a guarantee of the coherence of legal discourse. Objectivity is thus not merely a rhetorical tool but can be understood as an argument in legal reasoning.

The fourth section includes three related papers on the legitimacy of the judiciary in modern democracies. The first paper, 'Within Democracy's Reach? Revisiting Some Objections to Judge-made Law' by Tilen Štajnpihler, is concerned with the authority of judge-made law in a democratic state within the civil law tradition. He argues that two of the most common objections against judicial law-making, based on the separation of powers and democracy, are misguided. These objections cannot provide a sufficient reason to justify the claim that by making and following precedents, judges are neither making nor relying on *law* properly so called. Going beyond their traditional common sense interpretation, the paper argues that political and constitutional ideas of the separation of powers and democracy are in fact consistent with judge-made law even when precedents have more than persuasive authority. In the second paper, entitled 'A New Trend in the Debate on Justifying Judicial Review: Considering the Benefits of Judicial Reasoning', Ágnes Kovács contributes to the current debate in constitutional theory on the justification of strong judicial review. She argues, *pace* Waldron, that there are strong outcome-related reasons for giving priority to judicial reasoning over legislative decision-making in constitutional issues. Kovács suggests that the main reason why constitutional courts are superior to parliaments in deciding matters of constitutional interpretation is that as forums of public justification courts are unique and exemplary institutions of public reason. They provide the adequate framework for thinking about fundamental moral issues that arise in constitutional law. In a sort of educative role, courts can even have a positive influence on the quality of extra-judicial public moral deliberation. Finally, in his paper 'Between Reflexivity and Effectiveness. Dilemmas of Democratic Legitimacy of Constitutional Justice', Krzysztof J. Kaleta analyses the problem of power and legitimacy in a post-modern democratic political community, with special emphasis on the role of constitutional courts. Following Rosanvallon's theory of legitimation, the author claims that the authority of constitutional justice derives not merely from its effectiveness in guaranteeing human rights protection but from its reflexivity. Reflexivity should manifest itself in judges' efforts to create a broad spectrum of individual perspectives that are 'present' in the constitutional discourse of the community and make up the constitutional identity of the polity. He distinguishes between ethical and institutional dimensions of reflexivity and argues that the reflexive model of legitimacy can be maintained only if courts allow the people themselves to speak freely (ethical reflexivity), while also ensuring equal access to public deliberation (institutional reflexivity).

The fifth and last part consists of two papers on criminal law and policy. Both can be seen as case studies on how pragmatic or goal-oriented considerations confront with rights-based and principle-oriented arguments in the law of a constitutional democracy. In her paper entitled 'Shielding criminal justice from politics', Mojca M. Plesničar discusses whether and to what extent criminal justice can and should be separated from direct political involvement and public sentiments. Against the claims that such a shielding is necessary in order to reduce the punitiveness of criminal justice, the author argues that this view is simplistic: it overestimates the extent of and misunderstands the reasons for punitiveness and also the proposals for reducing it are unlikely to be workable. The second paper, 'Introduction of Criminal Law Powers in Other Legal Procedures: A Convenient Bypass for Obtaining Evidence?' by Sabina Zgaga, analyses Slovenian law on investigative powers of the state border and customs agencies from a comparative and constitutional perspective. She argues that compared to the strict human rights guarantees protecting privacy in criminal procedure, the extensive police power for searching persons and vehicles under the Slovenian State Border Control Act are disproportionate; the lenient rules on evidence collection also allow circumventing the guarantees of criminal procedure. Inspired by US and Strasbourg jurisprudence, the author explains how rules allowing for an efficient collection of evidence in non-criminal procedures can be in accordance with human rights.

Taken as a whole, this volume sheds new light on some important and topical discussions in contemporary jurisprudence and political theory. We hope that the readers find them inspiring and thought-provoking.

Finally, we would like to express our gratitude to the University of Greifwald, the University of Vienna, Pázmány Péter Catholic University, and the University of Debrecen for their generous financial support that has allowed the publication of this volume.

Lectori salutem!

Hull – Budapest – Kraków, April 2013

The Editors

Part I
Re-reading the Classics

The Relationship of Natural Law and Natural Rights: Organic, Contingent, or Logically Contradictory?

Szilárd Tattay

Introduction: two fundamental questions

Few would doubt the widespread commonplace in the history of ideas that natural rights were conceived from natural law. Nevertheless, the nature of the relationship between natural law and natural rights is far from being unambiguous. Although several competitive theories arose to explain this relationship, the debate around it has not come to an end.

It seems that the two most fundamental and most difficult questions in this regard are

(1) whether the 'encounter' between the concepts of natural law and natural rights in a certain period of the history of Western political and legal thought was necessary or merely accidental, and

(2) whether there is an organic, contingent, or logically contradictory relationship between these two concepts.

The relation between natural law and natural rights raises further issues as well. Is natural law or are natural rights entitled to logical primacy and is it possible to derive natural rights from natural law or vice versa? If above all obligations originate from natural law, what and how could establish a relationship between the norms of natural law and natural rights? Do natural rights only serve to fulfil obligations arising from natural law, or is their scope wider than this, and so and so forth?

In this paper I will try to answer only the two 'fundamental questions'. As it seems to me, these two questions are interrelated, and the answer to the first one is ultimately dependent upon the consideration of the second. The starting point of my argumentation is the statement that the 'intermediate period' between the thirteenth century, commonly regarded as the golden age of scholasticism, and the seventeenth century marking the beginning of modern natural law theory is essential concerning the evolution of the idea of natural rights. Thus the main reason why the problem of the relationship between natural law and natural rights is dividing historians of ideas and provides them with false ambiguities is that up to recent times they have neglected the thorough examination of these three and a half centuries between Saint Thomas Aquinas and Hugo Grotius.

Two diametrically opposed answers

There are two easily tangible, crystallised and characteristic opinions considering the historical relationship between natural law and natural rights. According to the first view, initiated by Leo Strauss and Michel Villey, there is a mutually exclusive relationship, or at least a fundamental tension and historical discontinuity between the ideas of natural law and natural rights. Strauss maintains that the authentic, classical tradition of natural law declined when (and not to a negligible extent because) natural rights arose. Modernity took over temporarily the concept of natural law inherited from Antiquity and the Middle Ages, but transformed it according to the axioms of modern philosophy, made it secondary and derivative compared to the concept of rights and finally abandoned it (see esp. Strauss 1953). Michel Villey is even more categorical. The French legal philosopher sees an absolute logical incompatibility between the ideas of natural law and natural rights, and claims that while the classical concept of '*ius*' meant the constraint of all power, the modern notion of '*iura*' means the theoretically unrestricted power of the individual (Villey 1975, 227–230).

The other general opinion is diametrically opposed to the previous one, as it regards the seventeenth-eighteenth-century modern variant of natural law rather than its classical version as a point of departure and ideal-typical (see e.g. Haakonssen 1996, Hochstrasser 2000). According to this approach, there is a close relationship and codependency between the ideas of natural law and natural rights. In this view, the most remarkable and imperishable merit of natural law theories is the elaboration of the idea of natural rights (see e.g. Péteri 1988, Gérard 2007). If we pursue this reasoning further, we may even arrive at the conclusion that nowadays, when jusnaturalism is considered to be a minority view in jurisprudence, besides its official advocates this approach endures latently – as a subterranean river – in the works of such human rights theoreticians as Ronald Dworkin, who cannot or are not willing to come to common grounds with natural law due to their dedication to analytical philosophy.[1]

1 Dworkin was even labelled as a natural lawyer; he wrote as a response Dworkin (1982).

The conventional story

In order to do justice between these opposite views, we have to examine at least the major stages in the history of the idea of natural law from the perspective of natural rights. Ancient theories of natural law are not taken into account, since neither Greek philosophers nor Roman lawyers knew the concept of natural rights; at least we do not have indisputable evidence that they did.[2] The concept of subjective rights founded on the immanent value of the individual could have been made compatible with Aristotle's metaphysical realism only with great difficulty, mainly because of his holistic approach subordinating parts to the whole.[3]

Aquinas who offered a paradigmatic formulation of medieval natural law theories only occasionally used the word '*ius*' in a subjective meaning. For him, *ius* is above all an objective concept, a synonym for '*iustum*', i.e. the object of justice, the primary meaning of which is the just thing or action.[4]

After discussing Aquinas's doctrine, the works that deal with natural law theories or the history of legal philosophy in general usually skip over or only briefly outline the legal thought of late medieval and Renaissance scholasticism and pick up the threads of the theories of natural law in the seventeenth century, with Thomas Hobbes (or maybe Hugo Grotius). It is exactly here that the books on the history of natural rights usually start (see e.g. Macpherson 1962).

Thus I continue my brief historical sketch with the author of the *Leviathan*. According to Strauss's influential thesis, Hobbes deduces the laws of nature from natural rights (Strauss 1952, 157). This thesis is widely accepted but questionable. While it seems incontestable that in Hobbes's political philosophy natural rights have priority over natural laws, it does not necessarily follow that laws of nature are derivative of natural rights. On the contrary, it seems that Hobbes himself excludes this possibility when he draws an impenetrable demarcation line between the concepts of 'right' and 'law':

> For though they that speak of this subject, use to confound *Jus*, and *Lex*, *Right* and *Law*; yet they ought to be distinguished; because RIGHT, consisteth in liberty to do, or to forbeare; Whereas LAW, determineth, and bindeth to one of

2 According to Richard Tuck (1979, 10–13), in late Roman Empire the words '*ius*' and '*dominium*' were often used in a meaning that in many ways resembles the modern concept of 'right'. Even if we were to accept this claim, it would not change the basic fact that Roman jurisprudence had no conception of universal natural rights inhering in all persons by virtue of their humanity (Tierney 2002, 392).

3 Fred D. Miller has argued in his monograph on Aristotle's *Politics* (1995, ch. 4) that the Greek philosopher had already used the language of subjective natural rights. His arguments, however, do not seem to be convincing.

4 I have discussed Aquinas's different usages of *ius* in detail in Tattay (2012).

> them: so that Law, and Right, differ as much, as Obligation, and Liberty; which in one and the same matter are inconsistent. (*Leviathan* ch. 14, 189)[5]

Hobbes consistently maintains this strict differentiation between law and right when he defines the concepts of 'right of nature' and 'law of nature'. According to his definitions, while the right of nature means the *freedom* to protect our own life, the law of nature *forbids* us to end our life, and also *commands* us to do everything possible to protect it.[6] If right and law are such incompatible concepts, then the laws of nature cannot be derived from the fundamental right of self-preservation. Although either the natural rights or the laws of nature can be deduced from our innate instinct to preserve our life, it would be rather difficult to posit an organic, if any connection between them.

On the other hand, since Hobbes does not require moral rightness as a conceptual element of natural rights, he excludes the possibility that they could be regulated or measured by the laws of nature. Thus natural laws cannot frame and restrict rights, the result of which is that in the state of nature 'every man has a Right to every thing; even to one anothers body' (ibid. 190). Moreover, it is doubtful whether the laws of nature are able to fit into this role at all, inasmuch as their normative status is questionable. Hobbes's point of view is rather ambiguous as to whether the laws of nature are commands expressing the will of the sovereign and omnipotent God, and hence are real laws, or merely 'theorems', 'conclusions' set by human reason in order to secure peace, which could only be called laws in a metaphorical sense (rules of the game, so to say).[7]

In his early Latin work on natural law John Locke takes over Hobbes's strict separation of law and right, law of nature and right of nature. As he claims, 'law of nature' should be conceptually differentiated from 'natural right',

> for right is grounded in the fact that we have the free use of a thing, whereas law is what enjoins or forbids the doing of a thing. Hence, this law of nature can be described as being the decree of the divine will discernible by the light

5 All references to *Leviathan* will be to C. B. Macpherson's edition (1982).

6 Ibid.: 'The Right of Nature, which Writers commonly call *Jus Naturale*, is the Liberty each man hath, to use his own power, as he will himselfe, for the preservation of his own Nature; that is to say, of his own Life; and consequently, of doing any thing, which in his own Judgement, and Reason, hee shall conceive to be the aptest means thereunto. [...] A Law of Nature, (*Lex Naturalis*,) is a Precept, or generall Rule, found out by Reason, by which a man is forbidden to do, that, which is destructive of his life, or taketh away the means of preserving the same; and to omit, that, by which he thinketh it may be best preserved.'

7 Ibid. ch. 15, 216–217: 'These dictates of Reason, men use to call by the name of Lawes; but improperly: for they are but Conclusions, or Theoremes concerning what conduceth to the conservation and defence of themselves; whereas Law, properly is the word of him, that by right hath command over others. But yet if we consider the same Theoremes, as delivered in the word of God, that by right commandeth all things; then are they properly called Lawes.'

> of nature and indicating what is and what is not in conformity with rational nature, and for this very reason commanding or prohibiting. (*Essays on the Law of Nature* 110–111)[8]

Later, in the *Two Treatises of Government*, he modifies his opinion and asserts that law not so much limits as directs free and intelligent human beings according to their real interests.[9] The true end of law is thus 'not to abolish or restrain, but to preserve and enlarge Freedom' (ibid. 306, emphasis omitted). On the other hand, Locke's concept of man as the 'owner of himself', which grounds natural rights, seems, in the final analysis, incompatible with his other fundamental argument that provides the basis for natural law, stating that man as God's creature belongs to God as His property. Consequently, in certain cases Locke has to give up, even if implicitly, the latter argument – for instance, by allowing suicide in certain cases (Zuckert 1997, 725).[10]

The alternative story

So far, our historical analysis seems to justify Strauss's and Villey's discontinuity thesis. The main reason for this might be indicated by the fact that modern natural law theorists were inclined to regard natural law as a sum of moral precepts that strictly prescribe or prohibit certain acts, thus impeding the individual's freedom of action. As a result of this formalist or legalist approach, they could not formulate natural rights on the basis of natural law, only parallel to the laws of nature, or rather against them.

However, as I suggested above, if we extend our study to the period between Aquinas and Hobbes (or Grotius), the problem of the relationship between natural law and natural rights appears in a different light. In his classical edition of the *Leviathan* from 1946, Michael Oakeshott was one of the first to warn that

8 I am using Wolfgang von Leyden's edition and translation of 1970. 'Haec lex his insignita appellationibus a jure naturali distinguenda est: jus enim in eo positum est quod alicujus rei liberum habemus usum, lex vero id est quod aliquid agendum jubet vel vetat. Haec igitur lex naturae ita describi potest quod sit ordinatio voluntatis divinae lumine naturae cognoscibilis, quid cum natura rationali conveniens vel disconveniens sit indicans eoque ipso jubens aut prohibens.'

9 *Two Treatises of Government* (Peter Laslett's edition, 1988) bk. 2, ch. 6, § 57, 305: 'For *Law*, in its true Notion, is not so much the Limitation as the direction of a free and intelligent Agent to his proper Interest, and prescribes no farther than is for the general Good of those under that Law. Could they be happier without it, the Law, as an useless thing would of it self vanish; and that ill deserves the Name of Confinement which hedges us in only from Bogs and Precipices' (emphasis omitted).

10 In the *Two Treatises of Government* (bk. 2, ch. 4, § 23, 284) Locke writes of the slave who, 'by his fault, forfeited his own Life' that 'whenever he finds the hardship of his Slavery out-weigh the value of his Life, 'tis in his Power, by resisting the Will of his Master, to draw on himself the Death he desires.'

> Hobbes was born into the world, not only of modern science, but also of medieval thought. The scepticism and the individualism, which are the foundations of his civil philosophy, were the gifts of late scholastic nominalism; the displacement of Reason in favour of will and imagination and the emancipation of passion were slowly mediated changes in European thought that had gone far before Hobbes wrote [...] the greatness of Hobbes is not that he began a new tradition in this respect but that he constructed a political philosophy that reflected the changes in the European intellectual consciousness which had been pioneered chiefly by the theologians of the fifteenth and sixteenth centuries. (Oakeshott 1991, 278)

Since then several books and articles have pointed at the medieval origins of the idea of natural rights – with different emphases and in different ways. Even if some of their statements seem questionable today, Georges de Lagarde's and Michel Villey's works were pioneers in this regard. Both French authors were convinced that the fourteenth-century philosopher and theologian William Ockham could be regarded as the 'father' of natural rights (Lagarde 1934–1946, Villey 1975).[11] Richard Tuck's *Natural Rights Theories* constituted a similar breakthrough in Anglo-American historiography. On the one hand, Tuck traced the concept of natural rights back to the revival of legal science in the twelfth century; on the other hand, he claimed that the first 'fully fledged' theory of natural rights was developed in the fifteenth century by the conciliarist and mystic Jean Gerson (Tuck 1979, 13, 25).

Research in this field has been definitely blossoming in the last decades[12] and reached its peak in Brian Tierney's and Annabel Brett's overarching, thorough monographs. Both discuss the continuous medieval evolution of the idea of natural rights in detail, from twelfth-century canon law to the so-called 'Second Scholasticism' of the sixteenth and seventeenth centuries (Tierney 1997, Brett 1997). We clearly get the impression from these works that modernity inherited not only the concept of natural law but also that of natural rights from scholasticism – and then transformed them into its own image. As Tierney pertinently noticed, 'if a doctrine of rights had not grown up in an earlier, more religiously oriented culture, there would, so to speak, have been nothing there to secularize' (Tierney 2006, 195–196). This picture fundamentally contests the common view that the idea of natural rights is a distinctively modern phenomenon that first appeared in the seventeenth century, as a political-legal consequence of the rise of modern science and market economy and the philosophical individualism of the age.[13]

11 See also Lagarde (1956–1970), Villey (1962), Villey (1964).

12 The main fruits of this blossoming are the following books and studies: McGrade (1980), Tierney (1988), Tierney (1989), Reid (1991), Pennington (1993), Mäkinen (2001), Oakley (2005), Mäkinen and Korkman (2006).

13 Perhaps the most prominent representatives of this view are – in their very different ways – Leo

But let us return to our original problem concerning the conceptual relationship of natural law and natural rights. According to modern deontic logic, a plausible way of grounding rights is to derive them from permissive norms (see e.g. Kalinowski 1964). However, the formalist approach of seventeenth-century natural law theorists, as we have seen, seems to exclude this possibility.[14] Medieval legal thinking, on the contrary, knew the concept of 'permissive natural law'. The essence of this idea is that natural law does allow and approve certain courses of action, without however commanding (or forbidding) them, and thereby gives freedom of choice to man – within the framework determined by the precepts and prohibitions of natural law.

Just like the idea of natural rights, the doctrine of permissive natural law has its roots in twelfth-century canon law, and was originally inspired by the problem of private property. Gratian's theory caused great interpretative difficulties to the Decretists. At the beginning of the *Decretum* Gratian gave a definition of *ius naturale* – taken from Isidore of Seville – encompassing both common possession and acquisition of things.[15] Then he attributed common property to natural law and private ownership to human positive law and custom, writing a bit later that human laws contrary to natural law are invalid.[16] It was Rufinus whose solution to this difficulty became the most widely accepted. He contrasted natural law commands and prohibitions with *demonstrationes* (indications), 'which nature does not forbid nor command but shows to be good', and classified common property only under the *demonstrationes* of natural law susceptible to change by human law.[17] It was another Italian canonist of the twelfth century, Huguccio, who developed this distinction further and thus introduced the notion of 'permissive natural law':

Strauss and Crawford Brough Macpherson; see Strauss (1953), Macpherson (1962). To take another illustrative example of this modernist standpoint, in Norberto Bobbio's book on Hobbes and the natural law tradition, we can also read that 'the theory of natural rights is born with Hobbes' (Bobbio 1993, 154).

14 Although Grotius and Locke sometimes refer to the permissive norms of natural law, these references remain sporadic.

15 *Concordia discordantium canonum* d. 1 c.7: 'Ius naturale est commune omnium nationum, eo quod ubique instinctu naturae, non constitutione aliqua habetur, ut viri et feminae coniunctio, liberorum successio et educatio, *communis omnium possessio* et omnium une libertas, *acquisitio eorum, quae celo, terra marique capiuntur*; item depositae rei vel commendatae pecuniae restitutio, violentiae per vim repulsio' (emphasis added). Isidore offered this definition in *Etymologiae* 5.4.1–2.

16 *Concordia discordantium canonum* d. 8 ante c.1: 'Nam iure naturae sunt omnia communia omnibus [...] Iure vero consuetudinis vel constitutionis hoc meum est, illud vero alterius.' Ibid. post c.1: 'Dignitate vero ius naturale simpliciter prevalet consuetudini et constitutioni. Quecunque enim vel moribus recepta sunt, vel scriptis comprehensa, si naturali iuri fuerint adversa, vana et irrita sunt habenda.'

17 *Summa decretorum* d. 1: 'Consistit autem ius naturale in tribus, scilic.: mandatis, prohibitionibus, demonstrationibus. Mandat namque quod prosit, ut: "diliges Dominum Deum tuum"; prohibet quod ledit, ut: "non occides"; demonstrat quod convenit, ut "omnia in commune habeantur", ut: "omnium una sit libetas", et huiusmodi. [...] Detractum autem ei est non utique in mandatis vel

> By natural law something is mine and something is yours, but this is by permission, not by precept, since divine law never commanded that all things be common or that some things be private, but it permitted that all things be common and some private, and so by natural law something is common and something private. (*Summa decretorum* d. 1 c. 7)[18]

The idea of permissive natural law soon pervaded not only canon law but also theology and was frequently invoked as a ground of natural rights. Its most detailed exposition was provided by the Spanish Jesuit theologian Francisco Suárez at the beginning of the seventeenth century.[19] For Suárez, permissive natural law plays a primordial role in the foundation of natural rights. Generally speaking, permissive natural law defines an area within which human persons can licitly exercise their inherent power of free will and free choice. More concretely, when natural law permits an otherwise intrinsically good act, 'it not only does not prohibit it, but since it is good, it also grants a positive faculty or licence, or a certain right to it.'[20] It should be stressed that for Suárez there cannot be a contradiction between the permissions and the precepts of natural law: permissive natural law can never permit or give right to immoral acts that are contrary to preceptive natural law. Thus the commands and prohibitions of natural law set bounds to the exercise of natural rights and prevent right-holders from abusing their rights (Tierney 2002, 401, 405–406). Finally, what is perhaps even more important, preceptive natural law obliges others to respect the rights conferred by permissive natural law:

> The right to all these things is natural, that is, they are all permitted by the law of nature. And in the same way the obligation of one person not to violate such a right of another is of natural law. (*De legibus* 2.18.7)[21]

---

prohibitionibus, que derogationem nullam sentire queunt, sed in demonstrationibus – que scil. natura non vetat non precipit, sed bona esse ostendit – et maxime in omnium una libertate et communi possessione; nunc enim iure civili hic est servus meus, ille est ager tuus.'

18 'De iure naturali aliquid est meum et aliquid est tuum, set de permissione, non de precepto, quia ius divinum numquam precipit omnia esse communia vel aliqua esse propria, set permittit omnia esse communia et aliqua esse propria et ita de iure naturali aliquid est commune et aliquid est proprium'. Cited by Weigand (1967, 353). It should be noted that Huguccio himself did not adopt the above 'common explanation'. Instead, he argued that natural law commands that everything be common (*communis*) only in the sense that private possessions are to be shared (*communicanda*) with others in time of need (Tierney 2001, 385 n. 16).

19 I have analysed Suárez's conception of permissive natural law and its organic relation to the traditional (Thomist) and subjective understandings of *ius* in Tattay 2011.

20 *De legibus* (Pereña edition, 1971–1981) 1.15.11: 'Nam quando permissio dicitur de actu alias bono, non solum non prohibet illum: sed etiam cum sit bonus, dat positivam facultatem, seu licentiam, vel ius aliquod ad illum.'

21 'Nam ius ad haec omnia naturale est, id est, haec omnia licita sunt iure naturae. Et eodem modo obligatio unius ad non violandum tale ius alterius, naturalis legis est.'

So Suárez attaches natural rights to natural law in at least three ways. First, it is permissive natural law that constitutes their normative basis. Secondly, the commands and prohibitions of preceptive natural law set limits to natural rights and ensure their lawful exercise. Thirdly, the same law protects natural rights against violation by others.

Conclusion

At the end of our investigation in the history of the ideas of natural law and natural rights we need to revise our temporary judgement and arrive at the following conclusion: Not only is there no necessary organic relationship between the ideas of natural law and natural rights, there is no necessary conceptual opposition between them either. While the tension between these two ideas was palpable in the modern, seventeenth- and eighteenth-century doctrines of natural law, it was essentially absent from earlier scholastic theories. On the whole, their historical encounter can be regarded as accidental, for it is possible to found a coherent theory of natural law merely on natural obligations. Nevertheless, under certain conditions they can complement each other favourably. The concept of permissive natural law provides a theoretical framework for such complementarity.

References

Bobbio, Norberto. 1993. *Thomas Hobbes and the Natural Law Tradition.* Translated by Daniela Gobetti. Chicago: University of Chicago Press.

Brett, Annabel. 1997. *Liberty, Right and Nature: Individual Rights in Later Scholastic Thought.* Cambridge: Cambridge University Press.

Dworkin, Ronald. 1982. 'Natural' Law Revisited. *University of Florida Law Review* 34: 165–188.

Gérard, Philippe. 2007. *L'esprit des droits: Philosophie des droits de l'homme.* Brussels: Facultés universitaires Saint-Louis.

Gratian. 1959. *Concordia discordantium canonum.* In *Corpus iuris canonici*, edited by E. Friedberg, vol. 1. Graz: Akademische.

Haakonssen, Knud. 1996. *Natural Law and Moral Philosophy: From Grotius to the Scottish Enlightenment.* Cambridge: Cambridge University Press.

Hobbes, Thomas. 1982. *Leviathan.* Edited by Crawford B. Macpherson. Harmondsworth: Penguin.

Hochstrasser, Tim J. 2000. *Natural Law Theories in the Early Enlightenment.* Cambridge: Cambridge University Press.

Kalinowski, Georges. 1964. Logique et philosophie du droit subjectif. *Archives de philosophie du droit* 9: 37–43.

Lagarde, Georges de. 1934–1946. *La naissance de l'esprit laïque au déclin du Moyen Age*, 6 vols. Paris: Béatrice.

Lagarde, Georges de. 1956–1970. *La naissance de l'esprit laïque au déclin du Moyen Age*, 2nd, rev. ed., 5 vols. Louvain – Paris: Nauwelaerts – Béatrice.

Locke, John. 1970. *Essays on the Law of Nature: The Latin Text with a Translation, Introduction and Notes.* Edited and translated by Wolfgang von Leyden. Oxford: Clarendon Press.

Locke, John. 1988. *Two Treatises of Government.* Edited by Peter Laslett. Cambridge: Cambridge University Press.

Macpherson, Crawford B. 1962. *The Political Theory of Possessive Individualism: Hobbes to Locke.* Oxford: Clarendon Press.

Mäkinen, Virpi. 2001. *Property Rights in the Late Medieval Discussion on Franciscan Poverty.* Leuven: Peeters.

Mäkinen, Virpi, and Korkman, Petter (eds.) 2006. *Transformations in Medieval and Early-Modern Rights Discourse.* New York: Springer.

McGrade, Arthur S. 1980. Ockham and the Birth of Individual Rights. In *Authority and Power: Studies on Medieval Law and Government Presented to Walter Ullmann on His Seventieth Birthday*, edited by Brian Tierney and Peter Linehan, 149–165. Cambridge: Cambridge University Press.

Miller, Fred D. 1995. *Nature, Justice, and Rights in Aristotle's Politics.* Oxford: Clarendon Press.

Oakeshott, Michael. 1991. Introduction to Leviathan. In idem, *Rationalism in Politics and Other Essays*, 221–294. Indianapolis: Liberty Press.

Oakley, Francis. 2005. *Natural Law, Laws of Nature, Natural Rights: Continuity and Discontinuity in the History of Ideas.* New York – London: Continuum.

Pennington, Kenneth. 1993. *The Prince and the Law, 1200–1600: Sovereignty and Rights in the Western Legal Tradition.* Berkeley: University of California Press.

Péteri, Zoltán. 1988. Az emberi jogok a történelemben [Human Rights in History]. In *Emberi jogok hazánkban* [Human Rights in Hungary], edited by Márta Katonáné Soltész, 21–49. Budapest: ELTE Jogi Továbbképző Intézet.

Reid, Charles J. 1991. The Canonistic Contribution to the Western Rights Tradition: An Historical Inquiry. *Boston College Law Review* 33: 37–92.

Singer, Heinrich (ed.) 1963. *Die Summa decretorum des Magister Rufinus.* Aalen: Scientia.

Strauss, Leo. 1952. *The Political Philosophy of Hobbes: Its Basis and Its Genesis*. Translated by Elsa M. Sinclair. Chicago: University of Chicago Press.

Strauss, Leo. 1953. *Natural Right and History*. Chicago: University of Chicago Press.

Suárez, Francisco. 1971–1981. *De legibus*. Edited by Luciano Pereña et al., 8 vols. Madrid: Consejo Superior de Investigaciones Científicas.

Tattay, Szilárd. 2011. The Subjective Concept of Right in Francisco Suárez. In *Legal and Political Theory in the Post-National Age*, edited by Péter Cserne and Miklós Könczöl, 7–17. Frankfurt am Main: Peter Lang.

Tattay, Szilárd. 2012. Are There any Natural Rights in Aquinas? In *Jurisprudence and Political Philosophy in the 21st Century: Reassessing Legacies*, edited by Miodrag A. Jovanović and Bojan Spaić, 11–22. Frankfurt am Main: Peter Lang.

Tierney, Brian. 1988. Villey, Ockham and the Origin of Natural Rights. In *The Weightier Matters of the Law: Essays on Law and Religion: A Tribute to Harold J. Berman*, edited by John Witte and Frank S. Alexander, 1–31. Atlanta: Scholars Press.

Tierney, Brian. 1989. Origins of Natural Rights Language: Texts and Contexts, 1150–1250. *History of Political Thought* 10: 615–646.

Tierney, Brian. 1997. *The Idea of Natural Rights: Studies on Natural Rights, Natural Law and Church Law, 1150–1625*. Atlanta: Scholars Press.

Tierney, Brian. 2001. Natural Law and Property: Gratian to Kant. *Journal of the History of Ideas* 62: 381–399.

Tierney, Brian. 2002. Natural Law and Natural Rights: Old Problems and Recent Approaches. *The Review of Politics* 64: 389–406.

Tierney, Brian. 2006. Dominion of Self and Natural Rights Before Locke and After. In Mäkinen and Korkman (2006), 173–203.

Tuck, Richard. 1979. *Natural Rights Theories: Their Origin and Development*. Cambridge: Cambridge University Press.

Villey, Michel. 1962. Les origines de la notion du droit subjectif. In idem, *Lecons d'histoire de la philosophie du droit*, 221–249. Paris: Dalloz.

Villey, Michel. 1964. La genèse du droit subjectif chez Guillaume d'Occam. *Archives de philosophie du droit* 9: 97–127.

Villey, Michel. 1975. *La formation de la pensée juridique moderne: Cours d'histoire de la philosophie du droit*, 4th ed. Paris: Montchrestien.

Weigand, Rudolf. 1967. *Die Naturrechtslehre der Legisten und Dekretisten von Irnerius bis Accursius und von Gratian bis Johannes Teutonicus*. München: Hueber.

Zuckert, Michael. 1997. Do Natural Rights Derive from Natural Law? *Harvard Journal of Law and Public Policy* 20: 695–731.

International Coercion and the Requirement of an International Rule of Law

Verena Risse

Introduction

The requirement of a rule of law seems to be intrinsically linked with coercive institutions and these coercive institutions constitute an inherent part of our understanding of the state. In other words: if what is to be ruled by law is a powerful actor, what other powerful actors are there if only states possess a monopoly of power?

On the ground of these considerations, one could be reluctant to consider that something like an international rule of law is conceivable. At the same time, we experience an ongoing shift of power from the national to the international sphere and see the group of international institutional actors steadily increasing. Against this background, the question of whether an international rule of law is necessary has been discussed for some time now and the positions defended seem to be anything but homogeneous. In order to shed light on the debate, this paper will contrast the positions defended regarding an international dimension of the rule of law with a Kant-inspired interpretation of its origins. In the first paragraph, I shall start by laying out why one might be sceptical about an international rule of law and go on by sketching the development of international institutions. In a second step, the positions defended in the discussion shall be presented and classified. Spelling out three interpretations of the rule of law on the basis of Kant's legal philosophy will be the object of the third paragraph. What follows from contrasting these considerations with regard to the international context will be assessed in the fourth and last part.

Defining the rule of law

Before I turn to analysing the more complicated case of its international application, it seems necessary to introduce at least a working definition of the rule of law. To begin with, the literal sense of the expression suggests that it is the law that rules. This can mean two things. It either means that the law rules the potent ruler with coercive powers at her hand which could potentially be abused. Or it means that the law rules instead of the ruler.

At this general level, there are at least two characteristics of the rule of law that deserve mention. First, it is traditionally assumed that the rule of law applies to the state and its institutional apparatus. Second, the rule of law can be divided into formal and material principles. Formal rule of law principles are meant to govern the action of the state and its institutions in a regulative or procedural fashion. Common contents of this are the prohibition of the retroactivity of the law, equality before the law or the independence of the judiciary. Material principles refer to the idea that the state's actions ought not only to be regulated, but that they should also be guided by substantial norms. Examples are values like equality or fairness or a specific set of rights that ought to be promoted. Ronald Dworkin famously distinguished between the 'rulebook' conception and the 'rights' conception, respectively (Dworkin 1985, 11). Traditionally, material emanations of the rule of law are better known in Continental conceptions such as *Rechtsstaatlichkeit* or *Etat de droit* than in their Anglo-Saxon twins. For this reason, Rosenfeld has described the relationship between the state and the law in the Anglo-Saxon context as 'antagonistic', whereas they are said to stand in a more 'symbiotic' relation on the continent (Rosenfeld 2001, 1319).

What these different models share, however, is the idea of regulating and keeping in check the state's use of power. This keeping in check may range between two poles. At the one end, one may find the idea of instituting the state and endowing it with a title to act. This characterisation corresponds to a liberal definition of the rule of law given by Jeremy Waldron. He claims that the rule of law is about the following relationship: states are only allowed to act when there is a rule, while individuals have a presumption of freedom unless there is a rule (Waldron 2011, 338). Here, the law rules the state's behaviour in that a rule is necessarily required for the state to act. At the other end, it means constraining the state's actions like the individual's ones in Waldron's example, i.e. the state is harnessed, but may act within certain limits. The practical truth probably lies somewhere in between, so that one could retain the following working definition: the rule of law denotes the fact of binding coercive powers on the ground of at least formal principles.

The international vs. the national realm

The idea of the sovereign state emerged since the Peace of Westphalia in 1648 and has dominated political thought until the 20th century. The core element of sovereignty is the 'supreme authority within a territory' (Philpott 2010) which is exerted internally and externally. The internal effectuation of this authority takes the form of, for instance, law enforcement by means of detention, the imposition of fines or police operations. The fact that there are no other actors endowed with anything resembling this monopoly of force implies that there is no institution similar to the state at the international or global level with an ultimate enforcement authority, either, i. e. there is no world government and no world state.

If one then assumes that the rule of law serves as a protection against an abuse of this unmatched endowment with power, there does not seem to be any good reason for setting up an international rule of law, since at the international level nothing comparable to state power must be controlled and kept in check by legal rules. Yet, there are two arguments that can be advanced against this first impression. First, even if the fact of letting the law prevail instead of brute force or political power constitutes the core idea of the rule of law, it has already been indicated that the conception, in particular in its central European manifestation of *Rechtsstaatlichkeit*, is broader than this. Secondly, the international order has seen an important development, too. During the last decades, more and more international organisations have been created and their fields of competence became increasingly specialised, diversified and went along with a substantive gain in power.

Some ideas from the research on international administrative law may serve as an illustration of this second point. In this relatively new discipline, scholars try to identify and classify the complex administrative structures of international law in a more nuanced and independent way in comparison to what used to be done before. In so doing, the aim is to find out where international organisations, states or regional entities fulfil executive tasks, how these are legally regulated and whether a new or different regulative or institutional framework is required. A preliminary definition of international administration reads as follows. International institutions perform administrative tasks when they 'operate below the deficit of highly publicised diplomatic conferences and treaty-making, but in aggregate they regulate and manage vast sectors of economic and social life through specific decisions and rule-making' (Kingsbury et al. 2005, 17). Examples include the United Nations High Commissioner for Refugees which has adopted different executive tasks in the field of administration and coordination of refugee policies, the World Health Organisation which is meant to prevent and control diseases, to which aim it issues worldwide warnings, or the Financial Action Task Force which has developed and now oversees a list of standards for the prevention of money-laundering (ibid., 21). The emerging international administration is an interesting case, because at the national level it is usually the administrative actors that command and execute state power. Therefore, identifying administrative law and qualifying different actors as having administrative functions at the international level may serve as an indicator for the location of coercive power, too.

An international rule of law

The question of whether or not the rule of law should be applied to the international context has been the object of debate for some time now and is usually answered in the affirmative. The views defended with regard to this international application of the rule of law, however, differ quite considerably. In particular, it appears that there are different meanings to the word international when it comes to the application of the rule of law. In order to get a grip on these different dimensions, it seems helpful to structure them along two lines. The first line refers to the scope or rather the level at which the rule of law is considered (i.e. national, supra-national, international etc.), the second one concerns the degree to which it is applicable (i.e. are only some elements concerned, is there need for the formal as well as the material criteria etc.). As an illustration, I will consider three understandings of the international spread of the rule of law.

An argument for a minimally international conception has been proposed, for instance, by Valérie Nádrai. Nádrai argues for treating the inner-state adoption of rule of law principles as a condition for states to become part of the international community. Her claim is based on a practical and a normative consideration. Practically, it is possible to demand the respect of the rule of law as an international standard, since there seems to be a wide consensus on its necessity. Normatively, Nádrai considers that states which are violating human rights internally also threaten the international stability, even if they submit their foreign policy to international standards (Nádrai 2003, 230). In this sense, the demand of the implementation of rule of law principles at the national level is merely a means to an end in the international realm, namely the condition for an entrance into the international community. And this international community is understood as a society of states only. The argument therefore leaves out the question of whether the rule of law should not only apply to states, but be extended to other institutional bodies which operate in the international realm as well.

A modest version of such an extension to non-state actors has been advanced by Simon Chesterman who argues for an international application of the rule of law, i.e. including international organisations, but only of its formal principles. Following his conception, formal elements of the rule of law ought to be observed in, for example, the above mentioned treaty deliberations. In particular, Chesterman argues for the government of laws, supremacy of law and equality before the law among the participants of international relations. He justifies this limitation with the argument that there is no worldwide consensus on a thick conception of the rule of law, yet the core principles he is proposing are almost universally endorsed (Chesterman 2008). It thus appears that Chesterman relies on an understanding of the international order as one in which states are not necessarily the only actors, but where the creation and regulation of other international institutions depends on the states' agreement. Therefore, the rule of law principles are tailored not precisely to the institutional characteristics or following the logic of the conception itself, but according to the more practical concern of whether they will potentially be applied and implemented.

The thickest conception, so to speak, combines a global dimension of the rule of law with an application of its material principles. This global rule of law binds all actors operating in the global sphere and is backed by certain normative considerations. A forceful proposal in this direction has been advanced in a recent paper by Jeremy Waldron who grounds his argument for an international rule of law on the claim that individuals must be the ultimate units of concern. This argument proceeds in two steps. First, Waldron shows that the classical analogy which compares the status of states in the international realm to the status of individuals in the national realm is flawed. Instead, individuals ought to be the ultimate object of concern for any legal system and thus in the international order, too. This connects back to the issue of international administrative law which regards states, in a line with other institutions, as performing the role of an international executive power. Secondly, Waldron claims that states cannot be entitled to the rule of law, for – by definition – they cannot fully seize the benefits of it. This is primarily due to the fact that the autonomy which the rule of law is meant to protect is nothing from which states can benefit, but which is inherently linked to the capacity of reasoning and making plans that only individuals possess. Instead, states, set up artificially like other institutions, are neutral in terms of ambitions and aims (Waldron 2011, 341). It follows that if the rule of law aims primarily at protecting the humane capacities of the individual, this seems to be equally pertinent at the international level when international actors gain in power and, even more so, when they have a direct impact on individuals. It has become clear that Waldron's interpretation of an international rule of law is a material one. Yet, as with all material interpretations, it depends on the material values defended whether or not it will be endorsed both at the national and at the international level. It will therefore be the object of the next section to focus less on a particular normative value, but on the relationship between coercive power and law which lies at the ground of the rule of law conception.

Back to the basics: The relationship between law and coercive power

In order to know where one is heading, it can be helpful to know where one is coming from. Following this premise, I suggest to explore the roots of the rule of law in order to understand the directions and developments it might take. The focus will lie on what has been identified as the core element of the rule of law, i.e. that it has something to do with the regulation of coercive powers. More specifically, I will propose to turn to the Kantian conception of the relation between right and coercion which has strongly influenced the liberal understanding of the rule of law doctrine.

To be clear, the notion of the rule of law, or rather *Rechtsstaatlichkeit* for Kant's linguistic context, only emerged at the beginning of the 19th century and was thus not yet existent at the time of Kant's thinking and writing.[1] Notwithstanding this fact, Kant reflects extensively on the relationship between individual as well as state coercion and the law in his legal philosophical writings. Kant's understanding of this relationship is marked by a two-staged argument of which the second part is better known than the first. This second part is the description of coercion as a 'hindering of a hindrance to freedom' (Kant, AA VI, 231[2]). It conveys an idea that is prominent in liberal justifications of state coercion. These justifications rely on the claim that state coercion does not actually constitute a threat to individual's freedom and autonomy, but rather – or predominantly – enables it by offering a reliable, foreseeable institutional context (e.g. Blake 2002).

This, as I said, only constitutes the second step of Kant's understanding of coercion and law and can hardly be read in isolation. The complementary element, so to speak, is the identity between having a right and having the authority to coerce. In other words, having a right goes along with having the authority to coerce. These rights derive their normative force from the innate right of humanity which every person possesses *qua* person and whose core is the right to freedom. It follows that the fact that rights go along with the authority to coerce is independent of the existence of or belonging to a society. Likewise, the exercise of coercion, at this very fundamental level, consists in the exercise and the assertion of each individual's freedom rights. Yet, if one person exercises her freedom, it is very likely that she thereby violates another person's freedom, i.e. that she penetrates the other person's realm of freedom, and thereby coerces this other right-holder.

Still, the interference must not be limited to the person of the right-holder, but can also concern the ownership of external objects that can be acquired in the state of nature. These acquisitions take place by affirmative acts and fall in the realm of private right. Yet, although the acquisitions can be rightful, they are not secure. Given these defects of the state of nature, Kant claims that there is a moral duty to enter a law-governed society (Kant, AA VI, 307). This idea of governance by law resembles the notion of a rule of law, but we will see that this is not the only dimension to the conceptualisation of the rule of law on Kantian grounds.

1 In fact, the first time the expression '*Rechtsstaatlichkeit*' is mentioned is in 1813 by Carl Welcker, while Kant deceased in 1804.

2 In keeping with custom, I cite Kant's works by reference to the Prussian Academy pagination.

Upon entrance into the law-governed society, new types of both right and coercion emerge. First, there are those rights that constitute the law-governed society. These are predominantly grounding and framing the society and its institutional set-up as such and might thus be considered primarily as regulative rules. Secondly, there are those rights that determine what must be recognised as one person's property – and this also extends to those acquisitions that could already be made in the state of nature, but only provisionally so (ibid., 312). The innate right to humanity, thirdly, continues to exist, but differences are to be made with regard to its internal and external part. The internal part is not concerned as both coercion and any societal form of right are external. The original external part, however, is given up in the moment of the constitution of the state and taken up immediately after it again. From this moment on, it is the external freedom of a member of a law-governed state (ibid., 315).

This leads to the question of the new forms of coercion that emerge upon entrance in the law-governed state. Coercion in the state is no longer individual coercion. The individual's authorisation to coerce, however, must probably be understood to continue to exist, but it is no longer exercised since the violations of freedom are meant to be stopped by the institution of the law-governed state. Therefore, the important new kind of coercion is that of state coercion which makes that rights are guaranteed and the mine and thine recognised (ibid., 312). State coercion is justified by the fact that it constitutes a 'hindering of a hindrance to freedom' (ibid., 231). In Kant's work, however, this idea is not explicitly reserved for state coercion, but seems to justify any coercion that is exercised in order to promote freedom (ibid.). Thus, in a sense the authority to coerce attached to the right remains, yet it is no longer exercised by the right-holder herself, but by the state which has been authorised by the individuals. With regard to the normative dimension, it is not clear whether this means that the individual authorisation has been given up in the moment in which it has been transferred to the state or that the state is authorised in a somewhat derived way and receives the constantly renewed authorisation from its citizens.

For the sake of completeness and clarification, finally, one might add that, according to Kant, punishment is not an instance of coercion in the sense of an effectuation of right as described. Instead, punishment constitutes a kind of *lex talionis* which is meant to reestablish the *status quo* or to function as revenge and which operates on different normative grounds (ibid., 332).

Having described the Kantian understanding of right and coercion, one might once again summarise what this could imply in terms of a rule of law. There are at least three readings of the rule of law that can be derived from the sketch of the Kantian conception just provided. The first one is a purely regulative understanding which refers to the kind of law that constitutes the state, but also to the rules that govern the state's exercise of coercion in order to hinder any hindrance to freedom. This variant would come closest to a formalistic interpretation of the rule of law. The second reading which is, arguably, closest to Kant's own intentions would imply a stronger focus on freedom and thus involve a material principle. Following this understanding, the state's actions ought to be governed by the aim to hinder any violation of and to promote freedom. This, indeed, liberal reading rejoins Waldron's position which focuses on the promotion of the autonomy of individuals. Yet, Waldron's statement also involves elements of the first reading in that he stresses that the state can only act if there is a legal ground for its actions which follows up on the idea of a necessary legal constitution of the state. A third reading lays the focus less on the aspect of freedom, but on the aspect of right and the authorisation to coerce that goes along with the fact of having a right and thus with the status of a right-holder. This implies that the rule of law concerns the practice and the conditions of the authorisation to coerce which is given to the state by the initial right-holders. The most important of these conditions might still be the material norm of enabling the individual freedom rights or rather all the regulations might still be given on the condition to promote the freedom rights to the biggest possible extent. Although this third interpretation seems to be rather similar to the second one, it differs in two important respects. The first difference concerns the force of the authorisation on which the whole construction relies, i.e. as long as an authorisation is given, the state may coerce; yet this authorisation can also be withdrawn. Secondly and relatedly, the fact of being a right-holder is meaningful, i.e. the status of a right-holder has a normative importance. It must be noted, however, that this last interpretation transcends the Kantian understanding in that his characterisation of the freedom rights is a moral and not a political one. While this one-dimensional character of the Kantian individual right has been the object of extensive criticism by Jürgen Habermas (1998, 121–123), I shall here contend myself by indicating that the last interpretation offered, although inspired by the Kantian system, goes beyond it. With these explorations of the Kantian grounds of the liberal conception of the rule of law at hand, one might once again turn to the question of its international emanations.

The international rule of law reconsidered

It will be the object of this last section to spell out what insights each of the three Kant-inspired interpretations can offer for our understanding of an international rule of law. For this purpose, it shall be referred to the first one as the regulative reading, the second one as the freedom-centered reading and the third one will be called authorisation-based reading. Before turning to the first kind, it shall be noted that it is perfectly imaginable to combine two or more of these readings. For reasons of clarity, however, I will confine myself to considering them individually only.

The first regulative reading corresponds to purely formal requirements of the rule of law in that it demands that the state, or more broadly speaking: any politico-institutional context, be law-governed. Unlike in the other two cases, it is not clear from where the normative imperative to this regulation derives, i.e. what triggers the demand to regulate such an institutional context. In the Kantian conception, there is a moral duty to enter the law-governed state, but this is to be seen in opposition to a state of nature. With regard to the international context, however, it seems as if this question does not necessarily need to be resolved. This is because the demand can be regarded as already applied to international institutions, insofar as they are constituted by legal norms, i.e. set up on the basis of legally framed contracts. The consideration, might play a role, however, in that it does not demand the creation of a world state, at least not as long as the individual freedoms can be guaranteed in the existent system.

The case is different for the second reading, i.e. the freedom-centered one. As already indicated, this can be classified as a material rule of law principle. Following the interpretation offered *supra*, the application of this principle would be demanded as soon as the individual right to freedom is violated, i.e. as soon as one person is coerced. Once such a violation of freedom occurs or is likely to occur, the demand to set up institutions that hinder such a hindrance to freedom arises. This also holds for the international context if there is specific need for international institutions to protect the freedom in an area which national institutions can no longer cover. Here, coming from the Kantian vision, the role of the institutions is functional, but they do not necessarily constitute a threat in themselves, for their use of coercion is always already wound up in the aim to which it is employed.

The third, authority-based reading seems to be remotest from the actual practice and how we conceive of the international realm. It is nevertheless not impossible to conceptualise its application. Indeed, this variant would demand the authorisation of individuals to the exercise of coercion by an institutional actor. This would imply that such an authorisation is also demanded for international institutions as soon as they intend to effectuate coercion. This element, I have suggested, is part of the status of a right-holder which depends only on the humanity of the person. It therefore constitutes a universal feature that is independent of any institutional context, be it national, international or global. Thus, in case any truly global institutions were set up, this requirement for authorisation would apply, too. Although the authorisation has some kind of legitimising function, it is not necessarily to be understood as a participatory or even democratic procedure. Rather, the authorisation for the exercise of coercion must come from those who initially possess it. These are the individuals who are entitled to be right-holders: they not only have the authorisation, but also the capacity to coerce – whereas institutions are merely artificial creations and thus have derivative coercive capacities and derivative authorisation to exercise them. In this conception, right so far only played the role of entitling in the form of individual rights. It could certainly be complemented by a broader legal system or law more generally.

What this analysis shows is that the three *foci* have different consequences for the reach of the rule of law. The regulative one is formal and international, yet only in its normative interpretation. The freedom-centered reading is material, international and even global to the extent that violations of freedom are at stake in either of the dimensions. The third authorisation-based understanding is rather formal or very minimally material, but global in character. Thus, whatever interpretation one follows, it demands that the principles of the rule of law be applied outside the state. This also means that it is not dependent on the choice of the approach, i.e. formal or material. Instead, each time it is the conception itself, and the underlying link between coercion and law, that imposes this expansion.

Conclusion

This paper reflected on the question of whether the rule of law can and should find application outside the state as well. The width of the views so far defended with regard to this question illustrates that the issue can hardly be regarded as settled. In addition, recent developments of the international institutional context which go along with shifting power to international organisations suggest to the least that the question of an application of the rule of law outside the state is not to be taken lightly. In order to escape the problem of applying a state-fitting concept to a non-state context, I suggested exploring the grounds for the liberal conception of the rule of law in Kant's legal philosophy. Working out its different elements allowed me to stress three considerations in more detail that constitute important interpretations of what the rule of law might be about without, however, tailoring it to a specific political order. Theorising the application of these elements to the international context, which has been the object of the last paragraph, showed that no matter which conception one is defending the stretching of the rule of law to the international realm is demanded. Thus, whether or not there ought to be an international rule of law does not depend on whether the concept which has initially been set up for the nation state can be transferred to the international context. Rather, it is the logic of the concept itself that demand its internationalisation.

References

Blake, Michael. 2002. Distributive Justice, State Coercion, and Autonomy. *Philosophy and Public Affairs* 30: 257–296.

Chesterman, Simon. 2008. An International Rule of Law? *The American Journal of Comparative Law* 56: 331–361.

Dworkin, Ronald. 1985. *A Matter of Principle*. Cambridge (MA): Harvard University Press.

Habermas, Jürgen. 1998. *Faktizität und Geltung*. Frankfurt am Main: Suhrkamp.

Kant, Immanuel. [1797] 1991. *The Metaphysics of Moral*. Translated by Mary J. Gregor. Cambridge (UK): Cambridge University Press.

Kingsbury, Benedict, Krisch, Nico, and Stewart, Richard B., The Emergence of Global Administrative Law. *Law and Contemporary Problems* 68: 15–61.

Nádrai, Valérie. 2003. Rechtsstaatlichkeit als Internationales Gerechtigkeitsprinzip. In *Kulturen der neuen Welt(un)ordnung*, edited by Georg Kohler and Urs Marti, 217–237. Berlin, New York: de Gruyter, 2003.

Philpott, Dan. 2010. Sovereignty. In *The Stanford Encyclopedia of Philosophy* (Summer 2010 edition) [http://plato.stanford.edu/archives/sum2010/entries/sovereignty].

Rosenfeld, Michael. 2001. The Rule of Law and the Legitimacy of Constitutional Democracy. *Southern California Law Review* 74: 1307–1351.

Waldron, Jeremy. 2009. Are Sovereigns Entitled to the Benefit of the International Rule of Law? *The European Journal of International Law* 22: 315–343.

Part II
Jurisprudential Methodology

The Subject Matter of Jurisprudence

Goran Dajović

Introduction

The topic of this article is the subject matter of jurisprudence, that is to say, the determination of the phenomenon that occupies legal theorists. I will only try to list a few, in my opinion, indisputable theses about the subject of jurisprudence, describe them and draw some methodological corollaries from them. I do not have any illusion that this would dissipate all dilemmas, but I believe that it is important at least to strive to do this. Why is it so?

There are at least three reasons to clarify this topic, namely to delimit the subject of jurisprudence correctly. The first one is professional: resolving this issue is a necessary condition for the existence of jurisprudence as a legal discipline. It is an old-fashioned scholarly convention that every legal discipline is determined by two elements. The first one is the subject and the second is the method of the discipline. For example, sociology of law is usually characterised by the method of empirical observation and its main subject, the relation between law and society. Criminal law has positively valid norms about criminal offences and punishments as its subject and the appropriate method for investigating such a subject is exegesis. According to this convention, it seems a pressing task for jurisprudents to determine the subject of their discipline.

The second argument for talking about the subject is practical. Namely, this question becomes important if we bear in mind a tight connection between the subject and the method of investigating this subject. It is some form of scholarly truism that the subject determines the method of its investigation, and that the proper tools and methods for researching phenomena depend on the nature of these phenomena. Likewise, the form of the concept of law (i.e. whether the concept of law should be a class concept, an archetype concept or perhaps a so-called folk concept or family resemblance concept) depends on the relation between the concept and the thing that the concept is a concept of. Consequently, in order to resolve these dilemmas about the concept first we must resolve the dilemmas surrounding the subject itself.

While asking the crucial jurisprudential question 'When one studies *the nature of law,* what *exactly* is one studying?', Scott Shapiro argues that 'getting a firm grip on this question is essential to understanding why it might be worth asking this kind of question in the first place' (Shapiro 2011, 4).

However, getting a firm grip is not possible without understanding the meaning of this question, i.e. what 'the nature' of something means and what, at least provisionally, 'law' means. If we want to know whether something interesting can be said about a certain subject, first we must determine what the respective subject really is. Therefore, if we want to answer whether jurisprudence matters at all, we first have to settle the question of its subject. How should we go about this job?

Every reflection about jurisprudence, just as about every other human artefact, can start with etymology, especially when there is an unbroken link between the current usage and the etymology of the word in question. As we all know, 'jurisprudence' is a word of Latin origin and literally means 'knowledge of law'.

Notwithstanding endless debates about the concept of knowledge or truth, it can be said that the knowledge of law includes knowledge of what the law is, that is to say, the nature of this phenomenon. Knowing the nature of law actually means having knowledge of those features of the law that make the law law and not something else.

Thus, many legal philosophers, including Raz, Dworkin, Coleman, Shapiro, generally and explicitly claim that the subject of jurisprudence is the *nature* (the essence) of law. For instance, Joseph Raz says 'a theory of law is a set of systematically related true propositions about the nature of law' (Raz 2004, 324). For all these reasons, in what follows I will assume that the subject of jurisprudence is the nature of law. However, this claim is laden with ambiguity and raises several important questions. Roughly speaking, the first set of questions is concerned with 'law' and the second with 'nature'.

Concerning the first question, it must be said that the existence of law is not without controversy. The reality of law is closely connected with the use of language and with the understanding of law by its subjects, i.e., with internal point of view taken by the addressees of law. This insight puts forward the problem of the relation between the word 'law', the concept of law and the reality of law as a phenomenon.

The second set of questions relates to the word 'nature'. When legal theorists seek to understand the 'nature' of law, this ambition constantly meets with the problem of necessity. This problem has two aspects. First, does necessity pertain to the concept of law, i.e. some necessary features of the concept, or does legal philosophy seek to discover necessary or essential characteristics of legal systems themselves? If the latter, another problem arises. The parochialism of legal orders does not seem to favour the generality and necessity of jurisprudential theses. The problem is whether there are any necessary features common to all possible legal systems and what necessity means in jurisprudence.

Let us now outline these two vital questions concerning the subject of jurisprudence.

'Law'

What is the first step toward the knowledge of law, i.e. in answering the question 'what is law'? Without doubt, first we must know what we look for and what we look at. Law as a phenomenon, which we look at, is not a natural entity. It is an artefact, albeit not quite like a hammer or a toaster. Law is rather a social and cultural product, and as such it is demarcated roughly by a certain social practice and ultimately by the participants' understanding and use of the concept-term 'law'.[1]

In order to explain the phenomenon of law almost all legal philosophers begin with talking about the entity which is commonly conceived and understood as law and about which people speak as law. In demarcating the phenomenon of law, the starting point is the social and linguistic practice of a certain community. In other words, it is the participants' understanding that serves to determine, at least initially, the subject matter of the observation. This is so because unlike the term 'gold' for example, which is a category whose boundaries are set by the world, in the same case of law, it cannot be said that 'the world' delimits what does and what does not count as an instance of 'law' (Bix 2003, 540). Actually, the use of language does it, at least roughly. I say roughly, because we could not *all* be really wrong about what it means for something to be law or about the proper use of the term 'law' in given instances. It is hard to believe that an entire community could get the law wrong and it does not know what the content of its law is. Such a broad misidentification is impossible in matters that are closely connected to people's attitudes.[2] Because of this, terms-concepts which denote certain social phenomena like justice, law or democracy, are not only the tools of science or philosophy for a better understanding of reality but are also, at least to some extent, part of reality itself (Raz 2004, 331).[3]

1 'There are at least two intuitions that must be preserved and articulated. The first is this: law is an intentional entity, or, to put it differently, an intellectual artifact. The second is this: the social and institutional aspects of law resist a purely mentalist account of it. A satisfying picture of the nature of law cannot drop either of the two' (Tuzzet 2007, 189).

2 '[T]o the extent that something is a purely cultural product, its reference consists in what people take it to be, which renders the possibility of extensive misidentification a logical impossibility' (Marmor 2005, 77). It is impossible to be wrong about something that has no independent ontological status.

3 As Leighton Moore says: 'The conceptual vocabulary we use to think about law often does not merely indicate legal phenomena but helps to constitute them. To ignore that vocabulary would be to ignore not merely a competing description but the phenomena themselves' (Moore 2002, 104).

However, I must add two caveats. First, jurisprudence does not take every use of the term-concept 'law' for granted, even if it is extensively accepted. One of the tasks of jurisprudence is to provide concepts which participants will be able to recognise as correct when they face them. Moreover, a good theory helps participants of a social practice to understand their practice better, and the better understanding of a social practice means a better understanding of ourselves.[4] Therefore, jurisprudence not only records the actual conceptual framework of law, but also scrutinises and reconsiders this framework.[5]

The second caveat is concerned, so to speak, with the non-conceptual side of the story about the subject of jurisprudence. Is there anything, besides our use of language, the folk concept and intuitions about law, which is a real phenomenon of law? And is this the subject of jurisprudence as well? The brief and obvious answer is that such a reality exists. First, language use or the use of term-concepts is a fact in itself. As I said, it is part of the phenomena which jurisprudence studies. Here, however, I have another kind of facts in mind. Namely, even if we do not have any idea about law, all of us can observe and accept that some normative systems exists and that certain human institutions and actions related to these normative systems exist as well.[6] Note that in this sense almost every jurisprudential theory is 'realist'. In general, almost every theory[7] purports to explain the phenomenon of law as a reality, that is to say, the theory tries to describe this reality just as it is, or rather as it presents itself from the point of view of the theory and its concepts (Weinberger 1991, 43–53).

We must ask the question: what is the nature of this reality? Does it have an essence or some necessary features? We must also ask whether these features exist at all, as necessary. I will try to answer these questions in the next section. Before doing that, I want to sum up what has just been expounded. The subject of jurisprudence is, so to say, twofold – first, it is the established folk concept of law: our intuitions

4 'A new concept of law, if widely adopted, might bring greater order and lucidity to the concepts and practices that make up our legal institutions by giving us an improved understanding (Hart would say "analysis") of what is specifically legal in our complex system of social rules' (Moore 2002, 98). See also Raz 1996, 221–222.

5 This point is much more complex than I am able to explain here. This complexity can be pregnantly described as follows. Legal philosophers always must ask themselves whether there are questions which participants in legal practice have not thought about or are puzzled about. One such question, for instance, would be whether courts are only law-applying institutions or sometime law-making institutions as well. Answers to such questions might not exist in participants' understanding, or might be seen as a puzzle or a matter of disagreement. On the other side, legal philosophers must not depart too far from the ordinary or common understanding of concepts, especially when they see that it is not confused or mistaken.

6 Actually, Hart has formulated it as 'the whole distinctive style of human thought, speech, and action which is involved in the existence of rules and which constitutes the normative structure of society' (Hart 1994, 88).

7 Except idealist theories, e.g. John Finnis's theory of law.

about law and in some way the conceptual framework of our legal thought. Second, it is a set of institutional and social facts which are roughly demarcated as such by the aforementioned conceptual framework.

'Nature'

Now it is time to clarify the second part of our question about the subject of jurisprudence, namely the question about the word 'nature' in the phrase 'the nature of law'. Searching for the nature of something is searching for the essential or necessary properties of this thing. However, in jurisprudence we face two separate questions or, broadly speaking, two kinds of necessity. The alleged necessity can be conceptual (logical) or empirical. The first refers to essential or necessary features of *our concept* of law.[8] But, as Jules Coleman suggests, the prevailing concept of law is not necessary in the sense that no other concept is logically possible. There is a significant difference between the claim that a particular concept is necessary and the claim that there are necessary features of an admittedly contingent concept (Bix 2003, 547). Necessity in the conceptual analysis of law is of a 'softer' kind, as it were. It only means that there are connections internal to the concept in question: *our concept* that is itself contingent is connected to a particular community and time (ibid., 549).

But we have to bear in mind that most 'things' have the nature which they have, regardless of whether we have concepts enabling us to refer to them. Thus, to discover the nature of law means to discover its 'necessary properties'. Necessary properties are those properties of law without which it would not be the thing of a specific kind as it is.[9] Does law have a nature in this sense, that is, some essential properties without which it would not be law? Does law have, after all, necessary properties which determine its identity as law? Or is law's existence, as Tamanaha used to say (Tamanaha 2001, 166), only a matter of linguistic practice and subjective understanding?

Doubtlessly, even as a social and cultural artefact, law differs from other social institutions by some distinct properties. This is the reason why we only understand and speak of certain type of institutions as institutions of law. Namely, we recognise some social institutions as institutions of law and some others as institutions which are not of the same kind. Sovereign states have legal systems and institutions of law, whereas the rules of a book club or the rules of etiquette are not legal rules.

8 'What then counts as an explanation of a concept? It consists of setting out some of its necessary features, and some of the essential features of whatever it is a concept of. In our case, it sets out some of the necessary or essential features of the law' (Raz 1998, 255).

9 Raz distinguishes 'those features of law which are general, i.e., shared by all legal systems' and the 'essential features of law, features without which it would not be law' (Raz 2001, 27).

There are certain features that every social institution or social practice, which is termed, recognised or conceived of as a legal institution or legal practice necessarily possesses. Consequently, there are institutions and social practices which share a number of essential features and which are necessary for these institutions being institutions or practices of law.

This raises a problem for every nominalistic approach to the concept of law. Such a description obscures the fact that the use of the term (for instance, 'the law') is governed by language rules which are successful, so to speak, only if the term is used regularly and repeatedly in similar situations. In order to achieve this regularity, language users usually pick out certain features, implicitly or explicitly, that constitute something as law. The conventional rules governing the use of the term 'law' condition its application (to a thing called 'law') on the instantiation of these features.[10] The task of jurisprudence is to explain these features, because they frame law as an institution of a certain type. In this way, jurisprudence actually works out a typology of institutions which rests upon the different essential characteristics of different kind of institutions.

Conclusion

Let me summarise what I have said so far. There is a folk concept of law and there are our intuitions about law: these are parts of the phenomena investigated in jurisprudence. This concept and the correlative understandings serve as the first step in the demarcation of law as a phenomenon. Law as a phenomenon is a real fact. The institutions of law, which are not a natural kind but social and cultural products, are the second but equally crucial part of the subject of jurisprudence.

Jurisprudents strive to get to the theoretical concept of law which best captures the necessary features of law as a phenomenon and which can diverge from our subjective understanding of law i.e. the folk concept of law.

10 In that respect, Ken Himma compares the term 'law' with the term 'bachelor'. It is worth citing the full passage where he is doing that: 'Law has conceptually essential features. This claim should not be construed as asserting that absence of certain features in a thing *absolutely* precludes the application of the term "law" to that thing regardless of the contingent practices governing the term's application. Rather, this claim should be construed as attempting to identify those features of law that ordinary usage presupposes are essential to law. Otherwise put, the claim that such features are essential to law should be construed as conditional upon particular – admittedly contingent practices of usage. Should those conventional practices change, the analysis of what is essential to law would also have to change. [...] An example would help to secure the point. [T]he term "bachelor" is a social kind because the status of being married or unmarried is determined by institutional social practices. Even so, existing usage conventions imply that the property of being unmarried is essential (in the sense being conceptually necessary) to being a bachelor. Though that might very well change in the future, such a prospect has nothing to do with the issue: current usage implies that being unmarried is an essential feature of being a bachelor' (Himma 2004, 733).

The first and the second theses imply that conceptual analysis is an indispensable method, especially in philosophy and the social sciences where, as I have just explained, concepts are part of the subject of the discipline. Like others philosophical disciplines, jurisprudence should neither disregard nor avoid building or reconsidering concepts, especially the concept of law, in favour of direct observation of the phenomenon.

The point of conceptual analysis is not to discover empirical truths about the world but to understand concepts about the world and about our understanding of it. To understand concepts means to discover or to describe their necessary features,[11] necessary in the sense previously explained. As a result, we can say that we also understand our society and ourselves better, which is the main goal in the analysis of so-called hermeneutic concepts.

This is the reason why Michael Moore is on the wrong path when he suggests that 'General jurisprudence should eschew [...] conceptual analysis in favour of studying the phenomenon itself, law' (Moore 1992, 206).

However, as the third thesis contends, it would be equally wrong to build a theory of law solely through conceptual analysis, without any reference to the empirical and social reality. This reality should remain a principal subject of jurisprudence. Paraphrasing Kant, we can say that 'perceptions without concepts are blind; concepts without perceptions are empty' (Martinich 2001, 2).[12]

I think that analytical legal theorists should not only be concerned with the features of the concept of law but should also be sensitive and responsive to the need for re-drawing such features in light of new experiences and new facts. The aim of jurisprudence should be neither only to explain the lexical meaning of 'law' and other terms of our conceptual framework nor only to demystify conceptual muddles in ordinary language. It is not enough to explain our concepts or the way we think about things: theorists must describe the thing itself, i.e. the features of

11 There is an essential challenge to conceptual analysis generally, which is grounded on a Quinean argument against the possibility of analytical truths (Quine 1953). This argument is extensively exploited by Brian Leiter who tries to replace analytical jurisprudence with a 'naturalised' one, i.e. with jurisprudence grounded in empirical methodology (see, e.g. Leiter 1999, 2001). The real impact of the idea of legal naturalism is relatively limited. Notwithstanding its correct insight about the importance of empirical investigations of legal phenomenon for jurisprudence, it seems that Jules Coleman is right when he defends the need for conceptual analysis against naturalism by pointing out that even 'the naturalized project can proceed only after a good deal of philosophical spadework has been done' (Coleman 2001, 213). There is an intensive debate about these questions in contemporary jurisprudence, but this debate is outside the scope of this article.

12 If Immanuel Kant's saying, 'Thoughts without content are empty; intuitions without concepts are blind' clearly illustrated the philosophical mind of the eighteenth century, today it seems that we could say, paraphrasing Kant, that philosophy without science is empty, and science without philosophy is (often) blind.

our institutions.[13] 'That task requires examining actual legal practices in order to ensure that one's statements about the nature of law respect social realities and do not mislead as to the facts' (Moore 2002, 98).[14]

Of course, this job can only be done through a concept which captures these observable features.[15] For, one should always keep in mind that a theory works through the concepts that concepts constitute a theory as, the words constitute language.[16]

Let me conclude by quoting a statement by Frederic Schauer:

> If we understand jurisprudence as the kind of theorizing about law that encompasses both the very idea of law as well as transdoctrinal and transnational features of law and legal thought, then jurisprudence's problem is how best to use the insights from various perspectives and disciplines to advance our understanding of the phenomenon of law. The concern [...] with which I sympathize, is not that the philosophy of law in the strict sense is or is not sufficiently empirical. Rather, it is that the potentially hegemonic tendencies of modern analytic philosophy of law will ignore or undervalue many genuinely important jurisprudential contributions that may not be strictly (or even not-so-strictly) philosophical. (Schauer 2006, 862 note 27)

It appears that my short report about the subject matter of jurisprudence confirms Schauer's words.

References

Bix, Brian. 2003. Raz on Necessity. *Law and Philosophy* 22: 537–559.

Coleman, Jules. 2001. *The Practice of Principle.* Oxford: Oxford University Press.

13 We should 'describe legal institutions rather than to make explicit what we already subjectively understand by terms such as "law" and "legal system". (Moore 2002, 93)

14 Moore points out that 'some readers might wonder whether a "description" of the "essential" features of something would be a conceptual or an empirical account. While I cannot argue the point fully here, I do not believe that a rigid distinction between conceptual and empirical propositions is helpful at the level of concept formation. At that level we are always in the intermediate position of examining phenomena and trying to capture their substantial differences in our definitions' (ibid., note 12).

15 'Is it not our aim to study the nature of law, rather than our culture and its concept of law? Yes and no. We aim to improve our understanding of the nature of law. The law is a type of social institution, the type that is picked up – designated – by the concept of law. Hence in improving our understanding of the nature of law we assume an understanding of the concept of law, and improve it' (Raz 2004, 331).

16 As well as words get their meaning in the context of rules of a certain language, as the concepts get their content only from the perspective of a coherent theory (Freeden 1996, 48).

Freeden, Michael. 1996. *Ideologies and Political Theory: A Conceptual Approach.* Oxford: Oxford University Press.

Hart, Herbert. 1994. *The Concept of Law.* Second Edition with a Postscript, edited by Joseph Raz and Penelope Bulloch. Oxford: Oxford University Press.

Himma, Kenneth Einar. 2004. Do Philosophy and Sociology Mix? A Non-essentialist Socio-Legal Positivist Analysis of the Concept of Law. *Oxford Journal of Legal Studies* 24: 717–738.

Leiter, Brian. 1999. Naturalism and Naturalized Jurisprudence in *Analyzing Law: New Essays in Legal Theory,* edited by Brian Bix, 79–104. Oxford: Oxford University Press.

Martinich, A. P. 2001. Introduction. In *A Companion to Analytic Philosophy*, edited by A. P. Martinich and David Sosa, 1–5. Malden: Blackwell Publishers.

Moore, Leighton. 2002. Description and Analysis in *The Concept of Law. Legal Theory* 8: 91–114.

Moore, Michael. S. 1992. Law as a Functional Kind. In *Natural Law Theory: Contemporary Essays*, edited by Robert P. George, Oxford: Clarendon Press.

Quine, Willard Van Orman 1953. Two Dogmas of Empiricism. In *From a Logical Point of View: Nine Logico-Philosophical Essays.* Cambridge: Cambridge University Press.

Raz, Joseph. 1996. *Ethics in the Public Domain.* Oxford: Oxford University Press.

Raz, Joseph. 2001. Two Views of the Nature of the Theory of Law: A Partial Comparison. In *Hart's Postscript: Essays on the Postscript to* The Concept of Law, edited by Jules L. Coleman, 1–38. Oxford: Oxford University Press.

Raz, Joseph. 2004. Can There Be a Theory of Law. In *The Blackwell Guide to Philosophy of Law and Legal Theory,* edited by William A. Edmundson and Martin P. Golding, 324–342. New York: Blackwell Publishing.

Schauer, Frederick. 2006. (Re)taking Hart, *Harvard Law Review* 119: 852–883.

Shapiro, Scott. 2011. *Legality.* Cambridge (MA), London: The Belknap Press of Harvard University Press.

Tamanaha, Brian. 2001. *A General Jurisprudence of Law and Society.* Oxford: Oxford University Press.

Tuzet, Giovanni. 2007. The Social Reality of Law. *Analisi e diritto*: 179–198.

Weinberger, Ota. 1991. Institutionalist Theories of Law. In *Controversies about Law's Ontology*, edited by Paul Amselek and Neil MacCormick, 43–53. Edinburgh: Edinburgh University Press.

Is 'Naturalised' Methodology in Legal Theory Helpful?

Luka Burazin

Introduction

According to the predominant methodology of legal theory, the concept of law is primarily determined on the basis of an *a priori* conceptual analysis and the intuitions of the theorist expounding his theory of law. The legal theorist uses introspection and leans on his own intuitions about the possible instances of law which he then takes as the basis for determining the essential features of law. However, the *a priori* character of conceptual analysis and the type of intuitions used in this methodological approach have recently been strongly challenged by Brian Leiter. According to Leiter, one should 'naturalise' legal theory in such a way that it be grounded in empirical research, which then enables an *a posteriori* conceptual analysis of the concept of law. In view of the fact that law is a concept 'people use to understand themselves', Leiter suggests that the introspections and intuitions of legal theorists be replaced by empirical research into the views of those subject to law, i.e. ordinary people's views about the law. Such a 'folk' view would represent the so-called internal point of view in the widest sense – the point of view of all the addressees of legal norms in a legal system who recognise these norms as reasons for their actions. However, since the concept of 'law' is an artefact concept, which does not allow for analysis in terms of its necessary or essential features, Leiter is also sceptical about the possibility of any intuition-derived knowledge about the 'essence' of law. It thus seems that the entire naturalisation project is, at least until some powerful social-scientific theory of law emerges, limited only to empirical investigation of 'folk' views about the law and some form of modest conceptual analysis.

In order to see whether legal theory could benefit from this kind of challenge, I will first briefly present a few introductory remarks concerning the subject of legal theory and then define the possible stages in the construction of analytical legal theory. Thereafter, I will outline how conceptual analysis works in general and how different kinds of conceptual analysis affect the object of our inquiry. I will then identify the various 'naturalistic' proposals Leiter has made over the years and, finally, assess the usefulness of his, as I have termed it, 'modest methodological naturalism' for analytical legal theory.

The subject of legal theory

Before embarking on the methodological questions of our enterprise, it is first important to determine its specific subject. As is the case with any other scientific discipline, the philosophy of science discerns the material and formal subjects of a discipline (cf. Glenn 1950, 4–5) or its extension and intension (Macan 1997, 18). The material subject of a discipline (its extension) is that which is also shared by other disciplines. In the case of legal theory, one could regard its material subject as the 'law' for 'law' is also the object of inquiry of other scientific disciplines (e.g. sociology, psychology, anthropology). The formal subject of a discipline (its intension) is the special perspective it provides on its material subject. In the case of legal theory, the special perspective it provides on the 'law' might be defined as giving an account of 'the nature of law'. For this purpose, I find useful Dickson's definition of analytical legal theory, which states that it 'is concerned with explaining the nature of law by attempting to isolate and explain those features which make law into what it is' (Dickson 2001, 17). In connection therewith she uses the phrase 'the nature of law' 'to refer to those essential properties which a given set of phenomena must exhibit in order to be law' (ibid.). However, depending on the endorsed methodological approach, the formal subject might also be defined as 'the concept of law'. This point will be addressed in the section 'Conceptual Analysis'.

Stages in the construction of analytical legal theory

The two main stages in the construction of a successful analytical theory of law are the following: 1) determination (identification) of the object of inquiry (Determination Stage) and 2) giving of an adequate account (explanation) of the object of inquiry (Explanation Stage). For the purpose of this paper, I will only discuss the first stage. The Determination Stage encompasses two substages: a) identification of samples (manifestations or instantiations) of law, i.e. examples of law by which the abstract concept 'law' is represented; and b) determination of the necessary, or necessary and important, or important but not necessarily necessary features of law. In the first substage the legal theorist should list the possible situations that could rightly be described as 'law', in the legal sense of the word. These could, for example, include state law, customary law, religious law, international law, transnational law, indigenous law and natural law (Tamanaha 2006, 224–230). The examples set out in this substage would then represent the samples or instantiations of law, on the basis of which the legal theorist should advance his analysis in the following substage of the Determination Stage. Building on the samples-of-law list, the legal theorist should then address the question of what features something must have in order to be added to his list of possible instantiations of law. Hence in the second substage the theorist determines the necessary, or necessary and important, or, as Schauer suggests, important but not necessarily necessary features of law (Schauer 2010, 3–4). These features could, for example, include normativity (Kelsen 2000, ch. 6 c, 43–47), coerciveness (Kelsen 2000, ch. 6 b, 35–43), a hierarchical system of norms (Kelsen 1951, ch. XI, 128ff), law's claim to be a legitimate authority (Raz 2009, 28–33), law as the union of primary and secondary rules (Hart 1994, 79–99), institutional character of law (MacCormick 2007), conventional foundations of law (Marmor 2009, 155–175), law's claim to correctness (Alexy 2010, 20–81), etc.

Here, however, one could raise an objection with regard to the sequential order of the two substages within the Determination Stage of our jurisprudential inquiry. As we have seen, according to the described sequence, the legal theorist first intuitively identifies clear and indisputable instantiations of law and, then, on the basis of these examples, determines their common necessary features. These features, in turn, serve as a means for considering whether there are some other instantiations of law that were intuitively, *prima facie*, disputable. Contrariwise, one could claim that the chronological order should be reversed – that the legal theorist should first intuitively determine the necessary features of law (i.e. determine when something counts as 'law') and then, on the basis of these features, pick out the possible cases of 'law'. However, when the sequence of substages is reversed some difficulties arise. First, in determining the necessary features of law one would have to start one's theoretical reflections with at least one clear case of law in mind. This would most probably be state law as it is the central and most unambiguous example. However, by confining ourselves to just one instance of law (i.e. state law), we would miss a whole set of other possible cases which could, it is at least to be assumed, represent adequate instantiations of law and be worthy of our theoretical attention. Second, if we start our inquiry into other possible cases of law by following a list of necessary features that is based on just the clearest instantiation of law, we might well come up against some sort of 'Gettier's problem'[1] and be prompted to revise our list each time this problem occurs. And it is most often the case when analysing, for exam-

[1] Gettier's problem stands for the giving of a variety of counter-examples against the standard definition of knowledge as 'justified true belief' by E. Gettier, which led to a long-standing debate about the adequacy of the standard definition of knowledge (Bunnin and Yu 2009, 283). I use the phrase here in its general sense to account for the giving of counter-examples against any preexisting definition, which leads to necessary revisions of this definition.

ple, international law on the basis of features of municipal legal systems that we are tempted to conclude either that international law is not law (which nowadays sounds implausible) or that 'law' does not have the features we attributed to it at the beginning of our inquiry. Third, as Coleman rightly suggests, in order to share the same concept we only need agree on a 'set of paradigm cases or instances of the concept' and not on the criteria of its application (Coleman 2001, 157). Therefore, since the agreement on a set of paradigm cases of law is a precondition for sharing the concept of law, which, in turn, is the basis for engaging in the reflection on the criteria of its application, it follows that the identification of a set of clear instantiations of law (paradigm cases) is a precondition for determining its necessary features (criteria of its application). Finally, experience has taught us that whenever we try to determine the essential features of some object in order to construct its concept, we first turn to (at least a few of) its possible clear manifestations in order to find their common denominator. Therefore, the identification of samples of law should precede the determination of the necessary features of law.

Conceptual analysis

Conceptual analysis is a philosophical activity of analysing concepts by identifying their contents and the way in which they relate to other concepts. Here I use the word 'concept' in its classical sense to refer to an idea (i.e. the content of our thinking) that applies to a set of individual things or situations, is expressed by words, 'mediates between the mind and physical reality,' and is of vital importance in our understanding (Bunnin and Yu 2009, 126). By conceptual analysis, it is claimed, the philosopher attempts to discover 'what elements a concept is composed of and how these elements are related' (ibid., 127), thereby defining the object of his inquiry.

In the traditional view, conceptual analysis is supposed to single out a set of *a priori* analytic truths about a concept that is being analysed, thereby revealing the necessary and sufficient conditions of its proper application (ibid., 127; Coleman 2001, 179). In the pragmatist view, which has some reservations about analyticity, it is not the necessary but, instead, the most salient features of a concept that we should be uncovering by conceptual analysis: 'those that figure most prominently in an explanation of the kind of thing it is the concept of—that are central to our understanding and appreciation of it' (Coleman 2001, 179). This is done by first identifying, on the basis of the philosopher's intuitions, clear cases of the analysed concept which then trigger further intuitions as evidence about the concept's necessary or salient features. Insofar as the philosopher's intuitions about clear cases correspond to the ordinary common understanding of the term by which a concept is designated, they reveal the 'folk theory' about things that fall under the concept (Jackson 2008, 31–37). Typically, the intuitions relied upon are those of the philosopher who takes them either 'to be representative of the intuitions of the class of professional philosophers' (intuition elitism) or 'of a broader class that includes non-philosophers—commonly referred to as 'the folk' (intuition populism) (Alexander and Weinberg 2007, 57).

Since concepts are seen as playing a vital role in our everyday understanding of various things and situations and as having the capacity to make the world more intelligible to us, the first aim of conceptual analysis is to provide a theory which yields a better understanding of the concept (Audi 2009, 100; Farrell 2006, 998). A better understanding of the concept ensues from a previously identified set of criteria for its proper use. In this way a theory of the concept disciplines the application of the concept and serves as the basis for analysing other possible instantiations of the concept that were not seen as its *prima facie* clear cases (Farrell 2006, 998–999). The second aim of conceptual analysis is to 'maintain a structure within which meaningful discussion can occur' so that we could know 'whether two people who appear to be discussing the same subject are in fact doing so' (Bix 2006, 51). Third, by employing conceptual analysis the philosopher also sets the boundaries of the analysed concept, thus making an investigation into its relations with other (neighbouring) concepts possible (ibid., 52). Finally, in determining the content of the concept through the use of conceptual analysis, it is supposed that we can 'learn something interesting, important, or essential about the nature of the thing the concept denotes' (Coleman 2001, 179).

As regards the last-mentioned aim of conceptual analysis one could raise the question of the real target of our conceptual endeavour, i.e. our ultimate object of inquiry. Is it our aim to elucidate *concepts* or to determine the *nature* of the objects they denote? Are we elucidating *ideas* or *reality*? In order to understand the difference, it is useful to invoke Jackson's dichotomy between modest and immodest conceptual analysis. In its modest form, conceptual analysis is given the role of 'addressing the question of what to say about matters in one set of terms *given* a story about matters in another set of terms' (Jackson 2008, 44). Modest conceptual analysis restricts itself to drawing conclusions about the content of the analysed concept and about how the concept relates to the folk conception of it (ibid., 43). It 'illuminates our concepts—our *talk*, as it were—not the referent we might have intended to understand' (Leiter 2007, 197). In contrast, immodest conceptual analysis goes on to draw conclusions about what the *world* which the concept strives to describe (i.e. the concept's referent) is like (Jackson 2008, 43–44). In its immodest role, conceptual analysis 'claims that analysing the way that we talk about, use and apply our concepts will yield knowledge not merely of those concepts themselves, but of what the world is like, i.e., of the reality those concepts attempt to conceptualise' (Dickson 2011, 485).

So what about law? Is the main task of legal theory to determine the content of the *concept of law* or the *nature of law*? Does it have to do with the *idea* of law or the *reality* of law? The answer to this question, it seems, depends on the form of conceptual analysis we endorse. The use of conceptual analysis in its modest role would determine our object of inquiry as 'the concept of law'. On the other hand, the use of conceptual analysis in its immodest role would determine our object of inquiry as 'the nature of law'. Therefore, we could claim that the methodological choice we make between the two forms of conceptual analysis also results in a difference in the formal object of our inquiry.

Methodological naturalism

An interesting challenge to conceptual analysis as the main methodological device in the construction of a theory of law is posed by methodological naturalism, advocated by Brian Leiter. For Leiter, in general, methodological naturalism in philosophy amounts to the view 'that philosophical theorizing ought to be continuous with and dependent upon empirical inquiry in the natural and social sciences' (Leiter 1996, 264; 1998, 81–82). It is 'a *methodological* doctrine about how we should approach philosophical inquiry' (Leiter 2009, 197). On this view, conceptual analysis and appeal to philosophers' intuitions are at best epistemologically limited methodological devices (Leiter 2001a, 366–370).

However, since Leiter's views on the range and role of naturalisation in legal theory and the epistemological (un)fruitfulness of conceptual analysis have changed over time, it is necessary to briefly outline his trajectory of thought in order to understand his present methodological position adequately and to assess its fruitfulness for legal theory.

The view that legal theory should turn to the naturalistic doctrine dubbed 'methodological naturalism' according to which 'theorizing should be continuous with *a posteriori* investigation of the sort found in the sciences' is introduced by Leiter already in his earlier articles (Leiter 1998, 103; 2001a, 368–370). In particular, he calls for naturalisation in legal theory which is to take the form of either Normative (Methodological) Naturalism ('normative theories, to the extent they are possible, ought to be constrained by and take into account relevant information from the sciences') or Replacement (Methodological) Naturalism ('to the extent normative accounts of the justificatory relation are impossible, we should aim for descriptive/explanatory accounts like those delivered by empirical science') (Leiter 1998, 103). However, in these earlier articles Leiter is firm in his belief that what should be naturalised is just the part of legal theory that deals with the theory of adjudication and not the whole of legal theory (Leiter 1998, 100; 2001b, 285). The reason for this is that in naturalising, e.g., the theory of adjudication, we might need to rely on some of the already existing theories of the *concept* of law (as Realists, according to Leiter, seemed to rely on 'a fairly crude type of legal positivism'), which are obviously the product of traditional philosophical methodology (Leiter 1998, 99–100 and Leiter 2001b, 284–285, 290–293). Leiter, therefore, claims that naturalisation still leaves room for non-naturalised legal theory, such as, for example, that which employs conceptual analysis (Leiter 1998, 99–100). He is, however, sceptical about the fruitfulness of conceptual analysis which amounts to the analysis of our 'law-talk' in order to achieve the goal of understanding the referential content of the concept of law, i.e. the understanding of law's fundamental features in the real world (Leiter 2001a, 358–359). Also, recognising the vulnerability of the claims of conceptual analysis when faced with the demands of *a posteriori* theory construction, Leiter attributes to conceptual analysis a merely instrumental role: 'if a proposed conceptual analysis is to be preferred to others, it must be because it earns its place by facilitating successful a posteriori theories of law and legal institutions' (Leiter 2001a, 368–369). Eventually, Leiter concludes that legal theory should 'get up from the armchair and find out what anthropologists, sociologists, psychologists, and others can tell us about the social practices in and around law' in order to provide a better account of how the (legal) world works (Leiter 2001a, 369).

In his later articles, Leiter takes an even more radical attitude towards conceptual analysis and philosophers' appeal to intuitions. Conceptual analysis and appeals to intuitions, he says, 'are epistemologically bankrupt' (Leiter 2003, 43–44) and a naturalised legal theory, 'aiming to describe the reality of legal phenomena, should [...] eschew such methods' (Leiter 2007, 183). He refutes even modest conceptual analysis, as set out by Jackson, for the reason that it is 'hard to distinguish [it] from banal descriptive sociology of the Gallup-poll variety' and from glorified lexicography, the results of which 'are strictly ethnographic and local' (Leiter 2003, 45–46). Since all claims could, in principle, be subject to revision in the light of new empirical evidence, there seems to be no room left for analytic truths as the proper domain of philosophy and, similarly, no room for engaging in traditional philosophical work, i.e. conceptual analysis (ibid., 44). Hence 'philosophy must proceed in tandem with empirical science, not as the arbiter of its claims, but as a reflective attempt at synoptic clarity about the state of empirical knowledge' (ibid.). Naturalised philosophy, Leiter claims, 'has no special methods for investigating the world; it is simply the abstract and reflective part of empirical science' (ibid., 50). In the case of naturalised legal theory, he concludes, 'this same approach would mean taking seriously the enormous social scientific literature on law and legal institutions to see what concept of law figures in the most powerful explanatory and predictive models of legal phenomena such as judicial behaviour' (Leiter 2007, 184). However, here Leiter already voices certain reservations about this way of naturalising legal theory given 'the epistemically feeble condition of the predictive-explanatory social sciences of law' (ibid., 192) and eventually, in response to Farrell, he subtly hints that he is ready to grant a small concession to the usefulness of (modest) conceptual analysis (ibid., 197).

In his more recent work, Leiter identifies three possible ways of naturalising jurisprudential questions. In addition to his already familiar project of naturalising the theory of adjudication, he now explicitly states two ways of naturalising legal theory that bear on questions about the nature of law. The first one involves turning to social-scientific accounts of law in order to understand the nature of law. With regard to this project, Leiter reiterates his doubts about the current predictive and explanatory power of the social sciences (Leiter 2009, 202; 2011a, 511). The second possible way of naturalising legal theory involves, according to Leiter, the use of the methods of experimental philosophy (Leiter 2009, 202–203). If we have concerns about the reliablity and representativeness of legal philosophers' intuitions and if 'folk' intuitions are to be decisive in fixing the extension of the concept of law, why not, he asks, 'investigate, empirically, what those intuitions really are,' namely 'what the "ordinary man" *really* thinks?' (ibid., 202). Since 'Raz himself emphasises that the concept "law" is one "used by people to understand themselves," adding that "it is a major task of legal theory to advance our understanding of society by helping us to understand how people understand themselves"', Leiter finds it 'curious' 'that no one has made any effort to figure out what "people" – as distinct from the subset of them who work in the vicinity of High Street – actually understand by the concept' (ibid., 203). Finally, Leiter calls for the colonisation of legal theory by experimental philosophy (ibid.). However, since Leiter rejects the view that the concept of 'law' as an artifact concept can be analysed in terms of its essential or necessary features (Leiter 2011a, 512–514; 2011b), he also doubts 'that there is any intuition-derived knowledge about the "essence" of the Hermeneutic Concept of Law to be had' and claims that 'fleeting, ethnographic knowledge about how the folk "around here" think about law [...] would be all that is on offer' (Leiter 2011a, 514) until some powerful social-scientific theory of law emerges (ibid., 513–514). I call this final formulation of Leiter's views about the current capacities of the naturalistic project in legal theory 'modest methodological naturalism'.

Concluding remarks: The usefulness of modest methodological naturalism

In spite of the fact that Leiter calls for the catching up of legal theory with 'naturalistic' developments in other branches of philosophy, most notably in epistemology, it seems that in the end he leaves us with just an invitation to combine a modest version of naturalism (by engaging in empirical research into norm addressees' intuitions) with modest conceptual analysis.

In contrast to 'pure' modest conceptual analysis, modest methodological naturalism substitutes philosophers' intuitions with 'ordinary' people's intuitions about law. If our concept of law amounts to our law-talk, people's intuitions should supposedly serve better in fixing the extension of the concept of law. Second, modest methodological naturalism regards conceptual analysis not as an *a priori* but as an *a posteriori* activity that follows our empirical investigations in order to correct errors which might occur there. As regards the subject of legal theory, there is no difference between modest methodological naturalism and modest conceptual analysis. Since Leiter holds 'law' to be a human artefact, empirically investigated intuitions can only provide knowledge of the concept of law and not of law's *real* nature.[2]

In the literature, some objections have already been raised against both the stronger 'naturalistic' idea of turning to social-scientific accounts of law in order to understand the nature of law (Coleman 2001, 210–216, 347–351; Greenberg 2011; Dickson 2011, 480–484) and modest methodological naturalism (Dickson 2011, 484–495). In practice, however, no serious attempt seems to have been made to date at verifying Leiter's final proposal. Such an attempt would need to show what 'ordinary' people have to say about possible samples of law as well as about the essential or at least important features of law, i.e. how those subject to law address questions stemming from the Determination Stage of our investigation into the concept of law (or law's nature). Still, a recent empirical inquiry (Burazin and Krešić 2012) and the preliminary opinion polls I did on my first-year seminar students do not seem to point to startling results that could improve our present theories of law. Quite to the opposite. The results obtained so far have only confirmed Dickson's remarks about the data collected by such empirical research (Dickson 2011, 493).

These preliminary empirical investigations, however limited in their scope, have shown that we should not expect too much from Leiter's proposal. It is likely that if, following his proposal, empirical research is done first, followed by an *a posteriori* conceptual analysis aimed at correcting errors, we could end up, to use Finnis's words, with a 'vast rubbish heap of miscellaneous facts' (Finnis 1980, 17). Perhaps better results could be obtained by reversing the sequence. Perhaps we should stick to the analyses of the concept of law based on our intuitions about the possible instantiations of law and law's important features and then engage in empirical research to verify whether our theories adequately reflect how those subject to law understand themselves by using the concept of law.

In addition, empirical research could also help us identify possible conflicts among our intuitions which, in turn, could be resolved by using further intuitions to

2 Despite certain views to the contrary, it is widely held that, in ontological strictness, no artefacts exist. It is believed that, as opposed to natural kinds, artefacts have no 'real nature' and no essence since their existence is mind-dependent, i.e. determined by human understanding and human interests.

adjudicate the conflict. These could provide 'positive theories for why certain intuitions should be included, and error theories for why certain rival intuitions should be excluded' (Liao 2008, 260). In this light, it seems plausible to view conceptual analysis and modest methodological naturalism as complementary philosophical enterprises. At the outset, however, we should seriously reconsider three questions concerning 'law'. First, is 'law' a Hermeneutic Concept? Second, is it capable of being decomposed into its essential features? And thirdly and finally, what is its 'nature' that we are trying to reveal given the fact that law is a human artefact?

References

Alexander, Joshua, and Weinberg, Jonathan M. 2007. Analytic Epistemology and Experimental Philosophy. *Philosophy Compass* 2.1: 56–80.

Alexy, Robert. 2010. *The Argument from Injustice.* New York: Oxford University Press.

Audi, Robert. 2009. *Epistemology.* New York: Routledge.

Bix, Brian. 2006. Conceptual Questions and Jurisprudence. In *Philosophy of Law*, edited by Brian Bix, vol. I, 48–62. New York: Routledge.

Bunnin, Nicholas, and Yu, Jiyuan. 2009. *The Blackwell Dictionary of Western Philosophy*. Chichester: Wiley-Blackwell.

Burazin, Luka, and Krešić, Mario. 2012. U kojoj mjeri hrvatski građani poznaju i vrijednosno prihvaćaju institucije i pravo Europske unije? Važnost empirijskih istraživanja za teoriju prava. [How Much Do Croatian Citizens Know About EU Institutions and Law and What Are Their Attitudes Towards Them? The Importance of Empirical Research for Legal Theory]. In *Poznavanje i vrijednosno prihvaćanje europskog i međunarodnog prava u Republici Hrvatskoj* [Knowledge of and Attitudes Towards European and International Law in the Republic of Croatia], edited by Ivan Šimonović, 85–108. Zagreb: Faculty of Law.

Coleman, Jules. 2001. *The Practice of Principle.* New York: Oxford University Press.

Coleman, Jules. 2004. Methodology. In *The Oxford Handbook of Jurisprudence and Philosophy of Law*, edited by Jules Coleman and Scott Shapiro, 311–351. New York: Oxford University Press.

Dickson, Julie. 2001. *Evaluation in Legal Theory*. Oxford and Portland: Hart Publishing.

Dickson, Julie. 2011. On Naturalizing Jurisprudence: Some Comments on Brian Leiter's View of What Jurisprudence Should Become. *Law and Philosophy* 30: 477–497.

Farrell, Ian. 2006. H.L.A. Hart and the Methodology of Jurisprudence. *Texas Law Review* 84: 983–1011.

Finnis, John. 1980. *Natural Law and Natural Rights*. Oxford: Clarendon Press.

Glenn, Paul. 1950. *Theodicy*. St. Louis: B. Herder.

Greenberg, Mark. 2011. Naturalism in Epistemology and the Philosophy of Law. *Law and Philosophy* 30: 419–451.

Hart, Herbert L. A. 1994. *The Concept of Law*. 2d ed. Oxford: Clarendon Press.

Jackson, Frank. 2008. *From Metaphysics to Ethics. A Defence of Conceptual Analysis*. New York: Oxford University Press.

Kelsen, Hans. 1951. *Opšta teorija prava i države* [General Theory of Law and State]. Beograd: Arhiv za pravne i društvene nauke.

Kelsen, Hans. 2000. *Čista teorija prava*. 2 izdanje [Reine Rechtslehre, 2. Auflage]. Beograd: Gutenbergova galaksija.

Leiter, Brian. 1996. Legal Realism. In *A Companion to Philosophy of Law and Legal Theory*, edited by Dennis Patterson, 261–279. Malden (MA): Blackwell Publishing.

Leiter, Brian. 1998. Naturalism and Naturalised Jurisprudence. In *Analyzing Law*, edited by Brian Bix, 79–104. New York: Oxford University Press.

Leiter, Brian. 2001a. Legal Realism, Hard Positivism, and the Limits of Conceptual Analysis. In *Hart's Postscript*, edited by Jules Coleman, 355–370. New York: Oxford University Press.

Leiter, Brian. 2001b. Legal Realism and Legal Positivism Reconsidered. *Ethics* 111: 278–301.

Leiter, Brian. 2003. Beyond the Hart/Dworkin Debate: The Methodology Problem in Jurispudence. *American Journal of Jurisprudence* 48: 17–51.

Leiter, Brian. 2007. *Naturalizing Jurisprudence*. New York: Oxford University Press.

Leiter, Brian. 2009. Naturalizing Jurisprudence: Three Approaches. In *The Future of Naturalism*, edited by John R. Shook and Paul Kurtz, 197–207. New York: Humanity Books.

Leiter, Brian. 2011a. Naturalised Jurisprudence and American Legal Realism Revisited. *Law and Philosophy* 30: 499–516.

Leiter, Brian. 2011b. The Demarcation Problem in Jurisprudence: A New Case for Scepticism. *Oxford Journal of Legal Studies* 31.4: 663–677.

Liao, S. Matthew. 2008. A Defense of Intuitions. *Philosophical Studies* 140: 247–262.

Macan, Ivan. 1997. *Filozofija spoznaje* [Epistemology]. Zagreb: Filozofsko-teološki institut Družbe Isusove u Zagrebu.

MacCormick, Neil. 2007. *Institutions of Law*. New York: Oxford University Press.

Marmor, Andrei. 2009. *Social Conventions*. Princeton and Oxford: Princeton University Press.

Raz, Joseph. 2009. *The Authority of Law*. 2d ed. New York: Oxford University Press.

Schauer, Frederick. 2010. Necessity, Importance, and the Nature of Law. Virginia Public Law and Legal Theory Research Paper No. 2010–19 [http://ssrn.com/abstract=1594930].

Tamanaha, Brian. 2006. *A General Jurisprudence of Law and Society*. New York: Oxford University Press.

Part III
Legal Reasoning and Objectivity

Objectivity as Coherence in Practical Discourse

Lidia Rodak

Introduction

Objectivity in law is one of the most discussed and least settled topics in jurisprudence. The literature is full of volumes dealing with the problems of objectivity[1] but nearly all are from a theoretical perspective. The lack of any theoretical consensus within legal scholarship also renders the discourse on the concept of objectivity rather opaque. Indeed, many authors who deal with objectivity create their own conceptual maps, offering their own typologies and understandings.[2] Although some legal scholars consider that it is better to use a specialised vocabulary when talking about objectivity in order to be precise and develop a better understanding, this may add to the confusion of the overall picture.

The concept of objectivity is fundamental both to the creation of law and its application. While its role in law creation is generally considered both necessary and a key function (Dworkin 1996; Moore 1992, 1985), objectivity in the application of law is commonly the subject of criticism and strong attacks. In this paper, I focus on objectivity in practical legal discourse in order to demonstrate that its role is much more complex than has previously been realised in scholarship.[3]

1 See Leiter (2002), Coleman and Leiter (1995), Coleman (1995), Greenawalt (1992), Kramer (2007), Marmor (2001), Patterson (2001), Pavlakos (2007), Postema (2001), Ripstein (1993), Stavropoulos (1996), Weinberger (1999).

2 Even the initial attempt to find a way to approach objectivity through dictionaries and philosophical encyclopedias revealed many different concepts which at first sight created a very confusing picture. One of them even identifies twelve different meanings of objectivity. See Judycki (1997, 404–406).

3 See Coleman and Leiter (1995, 331–349) who helpfully discuss this literature in detail. See also Minow (1986), Scales (1986), Singer (1984), Kennedy (1976), Crenshaw (1988), Delgado (1993). A short review of the arguments introduced in jurisprudential literature is the following: (1) Critical legal scholars criticise objectivity as a tool of rhetoric: the process of decision-making masquerades as deductive and non-personal, discretion as rule of law. Kennedy (1976) speaks of 'the pseudo-objectivity of the rule-as-applied' and Richard Delgado speaks of critical race theory's 'distrust of

This paper does not take for granted any of the existing theoretical perspectives on how objectivity should be defined or the necessary elements for its definition.[4] On the contrary, the description I am suggesting, based on an analysis of case law, is one of 'final effect': discursive objectivity created and shaped by legal practice. It deals with objectivity that is created bottom-up within the legal discourse and by the legal system, not one that is imposed from above. I will defend the thesis that objectivity is a necessary part of legal discourse at the levels of both legal assumptions and their application.Objectivity is treated as an argument in legal discourse; one that responds perfectly to the needs of the general character and demands of law. Its main role is to provide coherence to legal narration. The shape of legal objectivity is formulated by the internal dynamics of practical legal discourse, which in turn is determined by its character, demands and aims, and by the special requirements of legal narration. At the same time, the way objectivity is applied in practical legal discourse is influenced by the character of the objectivity of law itself, thus giving a particular meaning to legal objectivity that is domain specific.

Firstly, I will provide a general explanation of the method used in the paper. I will then introduce objectivity as an argument in practical legal discourse, supported by a list of examples. Finally, I will show the interrelation between legal narration and objectivity in order to demonstrate the double role of objectivity in providing both the convention that enables the application of law, and the coherence of legal narration.

Methodology: the bottom-up approach

The research behind this paper follows a *bottom-up* approach, looking first at practical discourse (law in action) prior to subjecting it to theoretical analysis. This model was designed to investigate the meanings of objectivity and the contexts in which they are used in practical legal discourse. By starting with the legal language of practical discourse rather than at the semantic level where a pre-organised layer of meaning already exists, the research allows to uncover both standard and non-standard uses of the term rather than just those which have already been nailed down. By analysing usage in this way, it is possible to examine the assumption of the open texture of language formulated by Waismann and Hart.[5]

law's neutral and objective facade'. (2) The Feminist Movement says 'objectivity masks inequality' because it plays the role of masking power relations in society. The Feminist Movement postulates a complete rejection of objectivity, describing it as a 'hypocritical notion'. See Harding (1993), Nussbaum (1992), Gilligan (1993), MacKinnon (1998), Minow (1986), Scales (1986).

4 For example, Postema's (2001) concept of discursive objectivity that is composed of many conditions, still presents a top-down perspective.

5 The 'open texture' of language refers to the potential vagueness of words under different circum-

Moreover, the application of the bottom-up model tackles the problems caused by: (1) the ambiguity of the notion of objectivity, and (2) the apparent inconsistencies in the ways it is used in the courts of law.

The bottom-up approach was carried out in two main steps. The first step was to compile a list of the meanings of *'objectivity in use'* taken from court judgments. The legal meanings of objectivity used in practical legal discourse were then analysed and carefully grouped into categories according to their 'family resemblances'. In the second step, we carried out further analysis of the data to examine the function of 'objectivity in use' in each instance.

The overall aim of the bottom-up model was to discover the special meaning of legal objectivity characteristic only for law, and determined by the context of the legal discourse, following Langacker's theory of cognitive grammar (Langacker 1987, 1991). The linguistic reconstruction of the meaning of objectivity is provided as the description of the 'family of resemblance' (Wittgenstein 2000 [1953]). As a result, one meaning of the term can fit more than one category. In addition, the list of categories is not definitive and categories are not mutually exclusive. However, since this part of the research is a hermeneutic activity aimed at verifying intuitions about the possible meanings of an ambiguous term (viz. objectivity), the lack of mutual exclusivity is not an obstacle.

The research takes into account both legal texts and the role of the interpreter in determining the effects of their interpretation. For this research, the interpretation was carried out by professional lawyers with a high level of linguistic and legal competence in their national legal systems. The actions of the interpreter are to a great extent influenced by culture, tradition, education, community and context. This raises the issue of the interpreter's idiosyncratic features or conceptual autonomy.[6] In order to tackle this potential problem, the methodology provides a common structure that prescribes for researchers how to determine meanings and how to settle the keywords.

---

stances. Inspired by Ludwig Wittgenstein's constructivist view on language, it was developed by Friedrich Waismann and then by H.L.A. Hart (1961, 120–132).

6 In the literature, these differences are characterised along a scale of *conceptual autonomy*. Certain aspects of the world can be conceptualised independently of other, more dependent aspects. For example, an event is conceptually dependent in relation to its participants. As Langacker (1991, 286) notes: '[One] cannot conceptualize an act of slapping without making some kind of mental reference to the entity doing the slapping and the one receiving it. The verb *slap* is thus described as referring schematically to these participants as salient facets of its semantic structure. By contrast, a person or physical object can be conceptualized independently of any event in which it might participate. They are, in short, conceptually autonomous. The same holds true for the complex world of ASL [American Sign Language] production, not only in conception [...] but also in representation that by its very nature must analyze signs into their component parts. This is precisely what an interface for conducting a search of an ASL dictionary must do. The ASL sign "my," for example, consists of (1) a certain hand shape (we call it Open-B), (2) moving toward, (3) a certain location (the signer's chest). Just as the participants to the event of slapping are conceptually au-

'Meaning in use' based on Langacker's cognitive grammar

As mentioned before, Langacker's approach was crucial for the objective of the research: to verify the special meanings of objectivity that are characteristic only for law and determined by the context of the legal discourse. Langacker (1987, 161–162) proposes that 'instead of regarding expressions as containers for meaning, we must focus on the symbolic correspondence between a phonological and a semantic structure.' So here we have a shift from the word to the notion, from the linguistic sign to the meaning determined by the interpreter. The interpreter accesses the meaning using his or her general linguistic and professional legal competences. A different popular approach utilises the conduit metaphor, where words are viewed as containers of meaning and where, if the words are accurately transferred from the speaker to the listener, the listener will be able to derive the intended meaning. In opposition to this, Langacker's usage-based model is constructed from bottom up. He assumes that users of language are autonomous, though they have a very similar network of conceptual notions. This network allows them to describe the degree of entrenchment of a certain notion in the structure of language and its extensions. The entrenched concept is expressed as a linguistic unit which can be easily and frequently encountered in usage. Extension is an atypical or novel usage which may become entrenched at some point but, for the time being, remains non-standard.

This methodology takes distance from the theoretical concepts of objectivity in law and focuses on examples within practical discourse. Instead of merely selecting understandings from a pre-designed list of possibilities drawn from theoretical discourse, this project adopts an approach in line with the idea of the 'open texture' of language. In this way, it seeks to identify how the concept is used in practical discourse and, from this, to ascertain whether or not there is a specific 'legal objectivity.'

It is vital at this juncture to note the contested nature of the concept of objectivity in relation to law. The field is one of contention, with the whole philosophical debate – from realist to post-modern approaches – failing to come to an agreement on a firm or core meaning of objectivity as a concept. The bottom-up model creates the possibility of arriving at a new legal meaning of objectivity specific to legal discourse. By investigating legal practice one can go beyond the settled schemes that exist in jurisprudential literature. The main benefit of this approach is that the results are independent from the theoretical scheme already determined in scholarship, and researchers are in open contact with the text of the law, and aware of its

---

tonomous in relation to the more dependent event coded by the verb *slap,* so too the "nominal" participants (hand shape and location) in the sign "my" are more autonomous than the "verbal" event of *moving toward.*'

contextual power. A bottom-up examination of objectivity also serves to reveal the difficulties inherent in a single understanding of objectivity: the epistemological approach reveals the impossibility of taking a 'view from nowhere' and provides a justification for the external observer. However, going beyond the theoretical schemes already described in literature does not mean going beyond every possible theoretical scheme. By doing interpretation within a legal context means that it corresponds to a legal paradigm, influenced and predetermined by legal thinking. This approach could also be described as hermeneutic, involving an extra-linguistic reality in the process of interpretation. This is based on the assumption that the legal text itself is only one of many elements supporting the interpretation (others include the interpretive community and the broader cultural community). Furthermore, the legal text itself transmits cultural, social, economic and political values. As Roger Cotterrell puts it, the interpreter has to take into account the contextual matrix (Cotterrell 1997, 13).

The advantage of this approach is that the research, in its contextual and anti-schematic dimension, has the potential to provide fresh results, different from what was previously known.[7] The main disadvantage of the bottom-up model is that, by focusing on language and what is directly named as 'objective' by the judicature, it cannot provide the full picture of the usages of objectivity in law, since focusing on language does not necessarily lead to a complete analysis of the phenomenon examined.

Objectivity of law vs. objectivity in law

Before proceeding, it is important to clarify some aspects of the use of the concept of objectivity in this paper. Firstly, a distinction must be drawn between objectivity *of* law and objectivity *in* law. The first concerns the conceptualisation of law, and the second practical legal discourse. Both are interrelated in that objectivity of law influences objectivity in law, and objectivity in law reshapes and influences objectivity of law. The character of this relatedness shows how objectivity of law influences objectivity in legal argumentation. The hierarchical structure of a legal system imposes the concept of objectivity from a top down perspective. The self-created authority of law makes this possible and enables legal decisions to be institutionalised. The accepted legal narration needs objectivity as a means of expressing and justifying its decisions.

As a consequence, there are different aspects of the ways objectivity is used in legal discourse. On the one hand, objectivity allows for the closure of the discourse and the non-recognition of subjectivity and particularity. On the other hand, 'ob-

7 Pilot research has already confirmed that the list of meanings of objectivity is much broader than what can be found in theoretical literature.

jectivity of law' is necessary for law because it enables the process of taking decisions by providing coherent justifications.

Summing up, top-down objectivity ('objectivity of law') influences the application of law, but legal practice also reshapes and produces its own aspect of usage (bottom-up objectivity or 'objectivity in law'). Top-down objectivity provides legal assumptions, while bottom-up objectivity provides coherence.

It will be argued that the objectivity of law is necessary at the level of basic assumptions about law (Postema 2001), and at least to a minimal degree[8] at the semantic and metaphysical levels (Rosati 2004, 275).

As regards the role of objectivity *of* law, there are different camps within jurisprudence. Both the natural law position[9] and the positivist approach claim that law is objective but they understand and define objectivity in different ways. Some authors, who do not identify themselves with a natural law position, stress that law can be understood as objective when everybody treats it in the same manner in the same situation (i.e. when law is equal for all its subjects) (Leiter 2002, 977–979). In other words, 'objectivity of law [...] in first line means that it is a normative order which is the same for everyone, independently of anyone's subjective attitudes' (Sieckmann 2009). Objectivity in law mainly concerns the decision-making process. There are three main spheres where objectivity is most often used:
(1) in connection with the decisions which are the effects of applying law,
(2) in connection with interpretative decisions
(3) in connection with decisions about fact setting (Wroblewski 1973, 150).

By objectivity *in* law, I refer to a practical perspective that is necessarily linked to subjects' actions and, consequently, is necessarily subjective. What we analyse here is legal facts in a practical context. Facts are ambiguous expressions of reality, dependent on the paradigm of interpretation (Nerhot 1990, 2). In exploring the meanings of objectivity of legal facts, the semantic-pragmatic approach has been adopted, largely following the conception of institutional legal facts in a narrative and normative context as developed by Neil MacCormick. According to this approach, institutional facts exist but, unlike brute facts, they cannot be perceived at a merely physical or psychological level. Facts such as 'contracts', 'marriage', 'money',

8 According to 'minimal objectivity', the view held by the majority of a relevant community determines what is right. Thus, if legal facts are minimally objective, they would be fixed by what the majority of judges take them to be; assuming judges are the relevant community. See Coleman and Leiter 1993, 549.

9 According to the natural law doctrine, the law is objective, firstly because it is given by nature, that is independently of people's wills and their influence on it, and secondly because the source of its existence makes law valid to everyone and everywhere. The content of natural law is also objective because it is simply given to people; their task is just to read what has been written for them and they have no influence on the material dimension of law. There are many different theories of natural law, from antiquity to the present moment. See Aristotle (1985), Thomas Aquinas (see Burns 2000), Hobbes (1994), Grotius (1990), Pufendorf (1994), Locke (1990), Finnis (1980).

'culture', 'knowledge', 'literature', 'parliament', 'sports', and 'games' exist but they need special rules in order to be institutionalised. These rules provide the meaning of institutional facts. The existence of institutional facts depends partly on brute facts, empirical events or behaviours, and partly on rules. This is why, according to MacCormick, such facts are dependent on human activity (MacCormick and Weinberger 1986, 24). 'Law and its facts [...] are rather products of communications as an encompassing process' (Broekman and Backer 2013, 103).

The next important feature of institutional facts is that they cannot be grasped or framed descriptively; they must always have a normative element. From the words alone, we could not understand what it means for people to get married, greet each other or play chess (MacCormick and Weinberger 1986, 24). We also need to know the normative element to grasp the meaning.

What follows from the institutional theory of facts for our considerations concerning the objectivity of institutional legal facts is that the definitive meaning of both brute and legal facts is determined in a particular context and is always partially dependent on subjective elements.

Objectivity as 'legal argument'

The success and popularity of objectivity in practical legal discourse can be demonstrated by the scale of its usage. It is used very often both by judges in the reasons given for their decisions and by the parties of the debate. This can be illustrated by the number of judgments in which the word 'objectivity'[10] or its foreign equivalents has been used. For example, in the Polish legal system a search on the keyword 'obiektywn*' yielded 82,542 judgments in the period between March 1927 and January 2012.[11] In the case law of the Court of Justice of the European Union (CJEU) a search on the keyword 'objectively*' yielded around 3,800 documents and searching on 'objectivity*' found 493.[12]

10 By using a keyword search on 'objectivity' and 'object*', it was possible to single out all the Polish court justifications in which the term 'objectivity' was used. This group of justifications was the starting point for further investigations.

11 The analysis is based on Polish case law published before March 03/2012 accessed from the System of Legal Information Lex Omega. Detailed research was carried out on 24.02.2012. This is currently the largest and most widely used electronic database of Polish court rulings. It is the basic research tool used by lawyers and opinion formers and is generally considered as a reliable information source. The search keyword was 'obiektywn*'. It enabled researchers to find all judicial decisions where the term 'obiektywność' (objectivity) appeared in various grammatical forms.

12 The analysis was carried out in May 2012 using the internet database at http://curia.europa.eu/. The latest 100 rulings issued by the Court of Justice, the General Court and the Civil Service Tribunal (only statements of the Court or Tribunal) were then selected for the purpose of further investigation. In 18 out of the 100 rulings the term 'objectivity' was only quoted by the parties or

To introduce the practical use of 'the argument from objectivity' in the process of decision-making, I draw on the results of a comparative research on objectivity in legal discourse,[13] introducing examples from the CJEU and the Polish legal system.[14] It is important to stress here that the use of objectivity as an argument does not represent all possible usages of the term in practical legal discourse.

In this section I briefly describe the situation where objectivity is treated as 'a legal argument'. By 'argument', I mean that 'objectivity' is used as a tool for constructing a legal discursive reality rather than to describe what already exists. In other words, this means that 'objectivity' is treated as a reason that determines the final result in an unsettled issue. This argumentative strength of objectivity seems to stem from the assumption of the objectivity of the law, which implies that what is legal is automatically considered objective in practical discourse. This observation was formulated on the basis of a number of examples where an argument is considered objective because it comes from a legally authorised person or text without any other justification, just as a 'last instance argument'.

By 'legal', I mean the use of objectivity in an argument in accordance with the specific rules of legal discourse and legal narration. What should be also noted here is that the legal character of objectivity and its argumentative power are interconnected.

'Legal usage of objectivity' has a special meaning and a particular role in legal discourse which is related to the assumption of the objectivity of law itself. The assumption of objectivity of law is taken almost literally in legal practice and what follows from this is that what is 'legal' is treated as 'objective' in practical legal discourse. This is expressed by the importance and strength attributed to certain types of arguments qualified as objective during the process of balancing arguments. This qualification as objective is delivered by law through its own authority. These arguments must also be introduced in legal (i.e. objectified) narration and can be characterised as syllogistic.

By analysing case law it is possible to identify the following groups of cases where objectivity is used as an argument:

1. The first group of examples are from cases where the strongest and the most valuable arguments are considered to be those based on legal authority. The argument from objectivity can be seen to come from various sources:
(a) legal rules;
(b) the legal order;

used in an applicable piece of legislation, rather than being invoked by the Court or the Tribunal. This left 82 relevant judicial decisions for analysis.

13 Objectivity in Legal Discourse: A Comparative Perspective. Research project supported by the Polish Ministry of Science and Higher Education (2010–12).

14 I will focus only on the argumentative use of objectivity leaving out other meanings and senses of objectivity that have been revealed during the research.

(c) legal dogmatics;
(d) descriptive argument, grounded in facts;
(e) arguments delivered by an impartial observer.

2. The second group of examples are cases in which objectivity is applied as a style of argumentation expressed as non-personal narration. Arguments introduced as impersonal rather than subjective are deemed more important. The standards of legal narration say that arguments must be inter-subjective and this is provided by accepted justification. Here, objectivity also provides argumentative power in a rhetorical sense.

Ad 1: Objectivity as legal authority. In these examples the legal phenomenon can be directly identified with its objectivity. This seems to be a consequence of the assumption of objectivity of law itself. The literal interpretation of the objectivity of law in practical legal discourse paints a picture where objectivity is the framework for the organisation of legal reality. In the legal world, objectivity of courts' and other legal bodies' decisions and actions is defined by the position from which these are taken. According to legal ideology, the position of the court ensures that it delivers impartial, just and objective judgments. Also legal rules and their content are assumed *a priori* to be objective. They all are identified as objective by law's institutional authority.

The legal meaning of objectivity seems to profit from its being derived from the authority of reason. In the history of philosophy, objectivity was first considered a realistic concept related to truth and the correct reading of reality. Although philosophy has now developed a much broader and more critical view, objectivity still holds to its claims of truth and correctness and, through this, gets its authority. Law needs to legitimate itself and its products. This is why it needs an authority that is self-created. Objectivity provides the essential supporting justification for that authority. As a consequence, the adjectives 'legal' and 'objective' can be treated as synonymous.

This group of meanings of objectivity contains commonly used arguments in legal discourse that are explicitly described as objective by the court. These include arguments from previously settled precedents, patterns settled in legal dogmatics, arguments introduced from a so-called impartial position, and scientific or logical arguments.

Ad a. The meaning of objectivity based on legal authority is mostly identified with legitimate sources of law, such as objective rules, an objective legal system, and objective criteria needed to make an objective decision. This is illustrated by the following phrases taken from case law: '*objective criteria defined by the legislator*' (sad apel. II AKa 13/08) ; '*objective because it is based on the legal rules*' (WSA II

SA/Po 656/08); *'objective because it is set by the court'* (NSA IV SA 1671/99); *'objective because it is set by the prosecutor's institutions/bodies'* (sad apel. II AKa 13/08); *'objective because it is in accordance with the objective legal order'* (WSA I SA/Po 656/08), defined in one reasoning as *'procedural and substantive norms'* (NSA IV SA 1671/99); or objective legal entities such as 'statute', 'objective law', 'legally enacted', 'defined by law', 'legally relevant facts', 'objective as coming from the legal order', 'objective as justified legally', 'on the basis of legal argumentation'.

As a consequence, it seems that law regards itself and all its products as objective (Coleman and Leiter 1995). It seems to be an *a priori* feature of law that is automatically applied to legal products. The following example from the CJEU (C-522/07 and C-65/08) illustrates the point: '[...] *according to settled case law, in the interests of legal certainty and ease of verification, the decisive criterion for the classification of goods for customs purposes is in general to be sought in their objective characteristics and properties as defined in the wording of the relevant heading of the CN and in the section or chapter notes.'* (See also CJEU, C-142/06, C-362/07). We can see here that the products of legislation are treated as objective. Their features are observable, verifiable features, but they are also chosen by the legislator, as are the criteria for their qualification. There are further features of the same products that are objective in the sense that they are empirically verifiable, but these are not listed in the legal act as objective. This means that the decision was taken at a meta-level, when the legislator decided which features to include.

Ad b. The second group comprises examples that treat objectivity in a legal sense as an argument providing justification. The objective justification in a legal sense can be identified with a rational reasoning. This may be reduced to the possibility of deriving the decision from the legal act, from jurisprudence of the court, case law, or any other legal source. Here is one example from case law: *'the second instance court replies to the pleas of lack of objective reasoning for the decision: the revised decision is objectively reasoned, is in accordance with the law, because it has been indicated by the relevant legal provisions.'* (WSA, III SA/Wa 2680/05)

Another example comes from the reasoning of the Constitutional Tribunal: *'The fact that the constitutional legislator placed the value of freedom of the press (media) in the first chapter of the Polish constitution means that this value is objectively justified and [...].'* (TK, SK 43/05). This fragment shows how legal values and their objective justification is constructed and interpreted by the Tribunal. The importance and also the legal meaning of this causation build an objective justification that is based on legal authority. Here it is argued that the first chapter of the constitution contains the most important values and, simply from the order given by the legislator, the argument is given unquestioned authority.

Other examples taken from the case law of the CJEU (C-246/08) describe legal definitions as objective. One finds, e.g., '*The objective nature of the concept of economic activity*'. An analysis of this definition shows that the scope of the term 'economic activity' is very wide but the term is objective in character in the sense that the activity is considered *per se* without regard to its purpose or results. Thus, as a general rule, an activity is categorised as economic where it is ongoing and is carried out in return for remuneration received by the person carrying out the activity (see CJEU, *Commission* v *Netherlands*, paragraphs 9 and 15, and C-408/06). However, the process of applying a legal definition changes its objective character. Although it is justified to assert the objectivity of abstract rules, it seems controversial to assert their objectivity in practice. Through the process of application, legal definitions become contextualised in a particular case. Maintaining that legal definitions are objective may be compared to persuasive definitions, which add force to arguments by means of words that provide a certain support.

Just like assumptions about the objectivity of legal rules and objective legal order, objectivity is also imprinted in the organisation of legal reality. This aspect can be shown by the following group of examples: CJEU (C-197/09) says that '*re-examination procedure [...] is an objective control proceedings, instituted without the initiative of the parties*'. This passage characterises the established objective position of the court in the legal system, where actions taken on the initiative of the court are called objective, unlike those motivated by one of the parties. It seems that the position of the court in these proceedings is objective by design. A similar situation is that of '*the harmonization rules laid down by Directive 85/374 as having the objective dimension*' (CJEU, C-358/08).[15] Here again the proceedings have an inbuilt objectivity.

Ad c. Concepts set by legal dogmatics are treated in a way very similar to precedents. Their argumentative power and prestige is derived from concepts developed by legal scholars and grounded in case law through the high number of citations. Arguments provided by legal dogmatics are also based on their authority. Some positions are accepted by the legal community as settled, while others, often polemical ones, are not.

15 'It should also be added that subjective elements deriving, for example, from the wrongful attribution, by the injured person, of the status of manufacturer of the allegedly defective product to a company which is not the manufacturer, or from the injured person's genuine intention to proceed against that manufacturer by way of its action against such other company, cannot, without infringing the objective dimension of the harmonisation rules laid down by Directive 85/374, justify the substitution, after the expiry of the 10-year period set out in Article 11 thereof, of that manufacturer in proceedings initiated during that period against another person [...]'

Objectivity in this sense may be defined as follows:[16]

(a) Patterns in legal doctrine that determine what is subjective and what is objective. Commonly used terms include 'objective and subjective responsibility', 'objective and subjective liability', 'sanctions', and 'constraints''.

(b) Objectivity identified with arguments based on authority as defined by legal scholars. Common phrases used in court rulings include: 'objective proof', 'objective evidence', 'objective as coming form legal norm', 'objective as confirmed by a legal body', 'objective evaluation – objective general clauses', 'objective liability, responsibility', 'objective interpretation', and other doctrinal concepts.

Ad d. This next group of arguments has a special importance in legal discourse. They are mostly identified with the arguments that are descriptive, truth stating, and grounded in ('objective') facts. Common legal uses of objectivity as the description of mind-independent objects in empirical reality are terms like *'provable'*, *'verifiable'*, *'measurable'*, *'real'*, *'factual'*, and *'empirical'*. However, as mentioned in the methodological section, in the legal world everything is legal and it is not possible to find something that is not embraced by a legal category, for otherwise it would be outside the legal world. The legal world is created through the language of the legislators. That is why even brute facts, which are not mentioned in legal statutes, are still considered in a legal context and will be involved in legal narration and may be qualified as institutional facts. As Weinberger stresses, social reality is penetrated by regulative and normative patterns and, because of these, the distinction between everyday reality and institutional reality is impossible in practice (MacCormick and Weinberger, 1991, 258). Lawyers do not refer to raw facts existing outside of any legal description. Life situations have to contain specific factors that can be designated by legal concepts only (Rigaux 1990, 48). This is how they become so-called objective facts.

Ad e. Arguments introduced from an objective impartial perspective or confirmed by the objective observer carry a strong weight in court judgments. The perspective of an external viewer who is not directly involved, not engaged personally, or has no own vested interest, is deemed to be objective. This standpoint is also taken by the judge deciding a case. Objectivity identified with the perspective of an external viewer (as a result of that individual's lack of personal involvement) can be also furnished by the independent position of the adjudicative body. An example of this is when a higher administrative body takes the decision as a controlling instance over a lower administrative body (NSA, II SA 534/98). Impartiality seems to be an

16 These examples are very common not only in the Polish legal system but also in the case law of other European countries. Full data are included in the final report of the project *Objectivity in legal discourse. The Comparative Perspective.*

inherent feature of legal decisions. It is formulated normatively in the rules of most legal procedures, which in turn provide order to impartial proceedings.

Ad 2: The objectified character of legal narration. The legal order has its own peculiar character. Legal narration has the structure of a public story, addressed to the collective (Jackson 1988 and Dworkin 1985, 425). Although decisions are mainly made in individual cases, they become part of the legal system and interact with the public. To complicate the situation further, the authors of the law (a collective body themselves) require judges – actually acting as co-authors – to take the position of the narrator, reading or applying the legal text. It is characteristic of legal narration that judges cannot speak for themselves, only in the name of the court. Another aspect is the accessibility of legal decisions by their potential recipients, hence the need for transparency and objectified language, which should ensure not only its comprehensiveness but also its acceptance. All these elements make the structure of legal discourse closely related to objectivity and we can observe an interplay between objectivity and law. Objectivity fits perfectly and recognises the assumptions of law: its public character, the requirement that judges make decisions based on law, justification of the decision in the name of the court, etc. Objectified legal narration applied by judges results in the specific use of objectivity and the specificity of using objectivity as a legal argument.

Objectified legal narration is strongly connected with the organisation of the legal world itself and especially with the general rules of legal reasoning. When the court considers arguments, it gives priority to those ones that can be recognised publicly, are supported by reasons that are confirmed and justified, and match the criteria used by a reasonable person rather than personalised criteria. By definition, the impartial court takes into account mainly the objective facts, not the subjective motives of the parties[17] – subjective motives must be objectively justified from the point of view of a reasonable person. Parties must deliver evidence for their behaviour to make their arguments convincing and credible. They should introduce their stories in objective not subjective terms. Through changing the narration, a particular individual becomes a legal subject and has to transform the empirical facts of the case into legal institutional facts. The legal subject needs arguments confirming his credibility in the legal world, so, to give a very basic example, seeing a doctor requires a certificate (Greenawalt 1992, 93–120). Some examples may illustrate this aspect of the organisation of the legal world.

In the following judgment (s.apel, I ACa 510/03) the Polish court claims that what is introduced by the party is just a subjective conviction, which cannot be con-

17 This is the most common perspective, especially in the public law, but one should stressed that in private law, the situations is different in some situations: subjective mistakes can be excuses in criminal or private law. subjective meaning matters in interpreting wills, etc.

firmed by an objective justification. '*The plaintiffs claim that placing the monument in the square lead to breakdown of their relationship with the art work, which is at most only their subjective belief, and objective justification cannot be found*' (WSA, III SA/Wa 2680/05).

In a decision of the Polish Supreme Court (SN, II CKN 465/98) we read that: '*feelings of the plaintiff do not have any objective justification and are not included in the accurate evaluation of the Court of Appeals. They are not sufficient to conclude that personal safety has been compromised or threatened by the publication of the disputed texts [...]*'

The character of narration and legal rules require that the court take into account only those motives that could be confirmed from the perspective of a reasonable person. The personal perspective is not recognised by itself, only by its confirmation in the institutionalised world. As a consequence, objectivity used as an argument in terms of law as a public phenomenon is mainly related to inter-subjectivity. So, objectivity is associated to social meaning, social standards, with objectivity understood as shared by the majority, what is common to all, as publicly known, or commonly accepted.

The rhetorical or persuasive use of objectivity is one of the common means to reach an argumentative aim and is firmly rooted in legal jargon. Terms like '*indisputable*', '*obvious*' and '*undeniable*' are frequently used to strengthen expressions. This rhetorical power of objectivity can be explained by the realist philosophical view of objectivity based on the dualistic division of what is objective and what is subjective. The presupposition is that whatever is objective has a strong, positive side and whatever is subjective has a weak, negative side (Raigrodski 2008). This strong account of objectivity is not context sensitive and so represents the values of stability, certainty, and truth, which legal practice readily adopts. The adjective 'objective' is very often used simply to emphasise or suggest the correctness of the choice and has a persuasive function. So much so that the often repeated phrase '*objective justification*' has become a permanent part of the legal jargon. Very often the term 'justification' is used on its own without any other adjective to explain the criteria for justificatory reasoning.

Even though legal narration has a public character, and is based on formal rules, it still requires transparency. As said already, the first requirement means loosing the subjective and individual recognition of legal subjects. This should provide for a transparent justification as part of the ideology accepted by lawyers. Objective justification provides grounds for the court to accept certain groups of arguments when taking decisions, as typified by the following expression: '*The Court considers it is not objectively justified*' (WSA, II SA/Łd 1086/02). But what kind of arguments are these? Looking closer at the structure of objective justification, it may be difficult to discern what makes a certain justification objectively valid.

I will investigate this question by reconstructing the courts' reasoning from their statements. Possible meanings of objective justification cover a very wide scale. They range from purely descriptive to purely evaluative, but most are a mixture of the two. Justification is based on very diverse criteria and supported by different types of arguments. Descriptive examples are confirmed by economic arguments or grounded in empirical facts, while evaluative ones are based on common acceptance or judicial discretion ('reasonableness'[18]). The diversity of examples may lead to the conclusion that almost any kind of argument can deliver objective support for the justification. Objective justification is then simply equal to justification, no matter what type of argument supports the thesis. Moreover, in some cases it is difficult to understand what objective justification means because the court just states that something is objectively justified without explaining why.

The need for objective justification in law is linked to the fact that objectivity excludes what is arbitrary and that it is part of an ideology accepted by lawyers. This seems to be confirmed by the declarations given by judges. To describe the function of 'objective justification',[19] one court can be quoted as saying that '*objective justification*' is used in order to exclude arbitrariness from the final decision (WSA, III SA/Wa 542/09). '*Objective justification*' is also introduced as an opposition to optional and discretional choices or decisions (NSA, II OSK 1287/06). However, objectivity in legal discourse can actually favour arbitrariness through closing the discourse by using last instance arguments that are not discussed or considered but simply accepted.

Conclusion

Objectivity seems to have a charm that lawyers very willingly take advantage of. As the examples introduced in the first and second sections show, there are at least three main characteristics of objectivity in practical legal discourse: its widely discussed persuasive power; its contribution to the legal ideology of "the objectivity of law"; and its ability to provide coherence in court deliberations.

In legal narration, objectivity plays a very special role, helping to hide the subjective voices of different legal actors. Incorporating subjectivity into objectivity is

18 The concept of reasonable person is an example of exercising judicial discretion. As posited by Judge Barak: '*When the judge describes a reasonable person, in most cases he is thinking of himself. Yet nothing could be further from the truth.*' Barak (1989, 125).

19 The term 'justification', because of its ambiguity, is variously understood. First as a thought process or as a result of the thought process of a set of linguistic statements which could be comprehended by the person who is not an author of the formulated justification. Procedural justification as a special case of argumentation is addressed to individuals who are intellectually critical. It must present a justified view as in accordance with accepted criteria for qualifying statements as true, judgments as right/correct and standards/norms as valid.

a necessary process but the extent of its involvement is not always openly shown. A judge is not only a narrator, or voice of the legislator, but also the co-author of a legal story. However, following objectified convention, judges conceal their own voices using accepted discursive tools. The negative side of using objectivity as a legal argument is the potential lack of recognition given to the subjects of law. In particular, by using general categorisations (e.g. reasonable person), the differences between individual legal subjects are neither personalised nor contextualised.

Alongside its great argumentative power, objectivity responds to the conventional requirement that all legal decisions be made and justified in an objective way. The negative side to this is that the use of arguments from 'objectivity' in legal discourse can sometimes be perceived as examples of exercising power through words[20]. Legal reality attributes the power and authority to legal bodies, not subjects under the law. There are many examples cited in this paper where 'objective' as an adjective is used to exclude other (subjective and therefore subordinate) arguments from the discourse. Law listens to objective criteria only, not to subjective voices in particular circumstances. It delivers decisions that are legal, taken on the basis of procedure, but not necessarily doing justice which can be recognised at a subjective level. The concept is imposed from above and is not negotiated. In this sense, it represents an imposed power expressed by words, where the judge has the final say. Objectivity is a last resort argument in exercising discretion to legal subjects who are upholding to the law. Objectivity plays a role in deciding what is right or valid, but from a position of power rather than through any systematic presentation of arguments. The hierarchical character of legal discourse makes arguments introduced as objective automatically stronger than others just because of the position from which they are presented. When decisions, evaluations, etc., are introduced as 'objective', no further justification is needed. Objectivity provides the easiest way to close the discourse and removes personal responsibility from the decisions taken.

However, objectivity is not exclusively a rhetorical tool in legal argument. It also fulfils the function of establishing coherence, which is a necessary condition for legal narration.

The short conclusion from this analysis of practical usage shows that objectivity is a very broad concept. It embraces all the meanings related to truth and correctness, as well as weaker forms of justification furnished by softer criteria, such as shared standards, common acceptance, and inter-subjectivity. It also introduces legal objectivity as a provider of coherence to legal narration.

[20] As some authors stress, the application of the notion of objectivity is necessarily linked with violence even at the subconscious level of language. See Zybertowicz (1995), Bourdieu (1991).

Legal objectivity that is shaped and re-shaped by legal narration is domain specific and in accordance with the demands of legal narration, the most important requirement being its coherence. Legal objectivity as coherence reveals the influences of the social and psychological framework of judicial bodies, who act in an institutional legal context, applying formal legal rules and, through discursive practices, make the final decisions.

Discursive legal objectivity plays the role of ensuring coherence between legal formalism, human activity, and social context. This is illustrated by the examples in the first section. The final decision must be taken according to the rule of law. As the examples highlight, the most valued arguments are those derived directly from law, where objectivity is based on legal rules, legal order, or legal dogmatics. This indicates the legal character of objectivity based on the internal structure of the legal discipline. Secondly, decision must be taken by an impartial judge, who is responsible for delivering an acceptable justification for that decision. The human aspect, which embodies subjectivity, is often hidden here, bracketed by the court taking a final decision. All these factors can be seen more clearly in the context of the final decision, which must be both valid and provide justice according to the authority of the law. In our analysis, the largest group of examples were those that had claims to truth or correctness, or were delivered by the facts themselves. What the law seeks is arguments that lead to 'one right answer' and objectivity is employed to justify this aim. What the court calls objective is very wide ranging, some instances could even been considered as conflicting.

Acknowledgements I wish to thank an anonymous referee for very helpful comments.

References

Aristotle. 1985. *Nicomachean Ethics, Book IV of the Eudemian Ethics,* trans. by Terence Irwin. Indianapolis: Hackett.

Barak, Aharon. 1989. *Judicial Discretion.* New Haven and London: Yale University Press.

Bourdieu, Pierre. 1991. *Language and Symbolic Power,* edited by John B. Thompson, trans. by Gino Raymond. Cambridge: Polity Press.

Bull, Hedley. 1990. The Importance of Grotius in the Study of International Relations. In *Hugo Grotius and International Relations,* edited by Hedley Bull, Benedict Kingsbury, and Adam Roberts, 65–95. Oxford: Oxford University Press

Broekman, Jan M., and Backer, Larry C. 2013. *Lawyers Making Meaning: The Semiotics of Law in Legal Education, vol. II.* Dordrecht: Springer.

Burns, Tony. 2000. Aquinas's Two Doctrines of Natural Law. *Political Studies* 48.5: 929–948.

Coleman, Jules L., and Leiter, Brian. 1995. Determinancy, Objectivity, and Authority in Law. In *Law and Interpretation: Essays in Legal Philosophy*, edited by Andrei Marmor, 203–278. Oxford: Clarendon Press.

Coleman, Jules L. 1995. Truth and Objectivity in Law. *Legal Theory* 1: 33–68.

Cotterrell, Roger. 1997. The Concept of Legal Culture. In *Comparing Legal Cultures*, edited by David Nelken, 13–32. Dartmouth: Aldershot.

Crenshaw, Kimberlé W. 1988. Race, Reform, and Retrenchment: Transformation and Legitimation in Anti-discrimination Law. *Harvard Law Review* 101: 1331–1387.

Delgado, Richard. 1993. The Inward Turn in Outsider Jurisprudence. *William & Mary Law Review* 34: 741–768.

Den Boer, Monica. 1991. Two in One Trolley: Reflections on the Relation between MacCormick's Institutional and Narrative Theory of Law. *International Journal for the Semiotics of Law* 4: 255–266.

Dworkin, Ronald. 1985. *A Matter of Principle.* Oxford: Oxford University Press.

Dworkin, Ronald. 1996. Objectivity and Truth: You'd Better Believe It. *Philosophy and Public Affairs* 25: 87–139.

Finnis, John. 1980. *Natural Law and Natural Rights*. Oxford: Clarendon Press.

Gilligan, Carol. 1993. In a Different Voice: Psychological Theory and Women's Development. Harvard University Press: Cambridge (MA).

Greenawalt, Kent. 1992. *Law and Objectivity.* Oxford: Oxford University Press.

Hart, H. L. A. 1961. *The Concept of Law*. Oxford: Clarendon Press.

Harding, Sandra. 1993. Rethinking Standpoint Epistemology: What is Strong Objectivity? In *Feminist Epistemologies*, edited by Linda Alcoff and Elizabeth Potter, 49–82. New York and London: Routledge.

Hobbes Thomas. 1994. *Human Nature and de Corpore Politico*, edited by J. C. A. Gaskin. Oxford: Oxford University Press.

Jackson, Bernard S. 1988. *Law, Fact, and Narrative Coherence.* Roby, Merseyside: Deborah Charles.

Judycki, Stanisław. 1997. Obiektywność [Objectivity]. In *Leksykon Filozofii Klasycznej [Lexicon of classical philosophy]*, edited by Józef Herbut, 404–406. Lublin: TN KUL.

Kennedy, Duncan. 1976. Form and Substance in Private Law Adjudication. *Harvard Law Review* 89: 1685–1778.

Kramer, Matthew H. 2007. *Objectivity and the Rule of Law.* Cambridge: Cambridge University Press.

Langacker, Ronald W. 1991. *Concept, Image, and Symbol: The Cognitive Basis of Grammar.* Berlin and New York.

Langacker, Ronald W. 1987. *Foundations of Cognitive Grammar. Volume I: Theoretical Prerequisites.* Stanford (CA): Stanford University Press.

Leiter, Brian. 2002. Law and Objectivity. In *The Oxford Handbook of Jurisprudence and Philosophy of Law*, edited by Jules Coleman, and Scott Shapiro, 969–989. Oxford: Oxford University Press.

Locke, John. 1990. *Questions Concerning the Law of Nature*, edited by Robert Horwitz. Cornell University Press: Ithaca (NY).

MacCormick, Neil, and Weinberger, Ota. 1986. *An Institutional Theory of Law.* Dordrecht: Kluwer.

MacCormick, Neil, and Weinberger, Ota. 1985. *Grundlagen des institutionalistischen Rechtspositivimus.* Berlin: Duncker & Humblot.

MacKinnon, Catherine A. 1998. Difference and Dominance: on Sex Discrimination. In *Sourcebook on Feminist Jurisprudence*, edited by Hillaire Burnett, 211–221. London, Sydney: Cavendish.

Marmor, Andrei. 2001. *Positive Law and Objective Values.* Oxford: Clarendon Press.

Minow, Martha. 1986. Justice Engendered. *Harvard Law Review* 101: 10–127.

Moore, Michael S. 1992. Moral Reality Revisited. *Michigan Law Review* 90: 2424–2533.

Moore Michael S. 1985. A Natural Law Theory of Interpretation. *Southern California Law Review* 58: 277–398.

Nerhot, Patrick. 1990. Introduction. In *Law, Interpretation, and Reality: Essays in Epistemology, Hermeneutics and Jurisprudence*, edited by Patrick Nerhot, 1–10. Kluwer: Dordrecht.

Nussbaum, Martha C. 1992. Human Functioning and Social Justice: In Defense of Aristotelian Essentialism. *Political Theory* 20: 202–246.

Patterson, Dennis. 2001. Normativity and Objectivity in Law. *William & Marry Law Review* 43: 325–363.

Pavlakos, George. 2007. *Our Knowledge of Law: Objectivity and Practice in Legal Theory.* Oxford and Portland, Oregon: Hart Publishing.

Postema, Gerald. 2001. Objectivity Fit for Law. In *Objectivity in Law and Morals*, edited by Brian Leiter, 99–143. Cambridge: Cambridge University Press.

Rosati, Connie S. 2004. Some Puzzles about the Objectivity of Law. *Law and Philosophy* 23: 273–323.

Raigrodski, Dana. 2008. Reasonableness and Objectivity: A Feminist Discourse of the Fourth Amendment. *Texas Journal of Women & the Law* 17: 153–226.

Rigaux, François. 1990. The Concept of Fact in Legal Science. In *Law, Interpretation and Reality: Essays in Epistemology, Hermeneutics and the Human Sciences*, edited by Patrick Nerhot, 38–49. Dordrecht: Kluwer.

Ripstein, Arthur. 1993. Questionable Objectivity. *Noûs* 27.3: 355–372.

Sieckmann, Jan. 2009. Objectivity of Law. In *IVR Encyclopaedia of Jurisprudence, Legal Theory and Philosophy of Law* [http://www.ivr-enc.info/en/entry.php?what=showEntry&entryId=43].

Stavropoulos, Nicos. 1996. *Objectivity in Law.* Oxford: Clarendon Press.

Scales, Ann C. 1986. The Emergence of Feminist Jurisprudence: An Essay. *Yale Law Journal* 95: 1373–1403.

Singer, Joseph W. 1984. The Player and the Cards: Nihilism and Legal Theory. *Yale Law Journal* 94: 1–70.

Sen, Amartya. 1993. Positional Objectivity. *Philosophy & Public Affairs* 22: 126–145.

Pufendorf, Samuel von. 1994. *The Political Writings of Samuel Pufendorf*, edited by Craig L. Carr. New York: Oxford University Press.

Weinberger, Ota. 1999. Objectivity and Rationality in Lawyer's Reasoning. In *Theory of Legal Science*, edited by Aleksander Peczenik, Lars Lindahl, and Bert van Roermund, 217–234. Dordrecht: Reidel.

Wittgenstein, Ludwig. 2000 [1953]. *Dociekania Filozoficzne [Philosophical Investigations]*, trans by B. Wolniewicz. Warszawa: PWN.

Wróblewski, J. 1973. *Wartości a decyzja sądowa [Law-making and hierarchies of values].* Wrocław–Warszawa–Kraków–Gdańsk: Zakład Narodowy im. Ossolińskich.

Zybertowicz, Andrzej, 1995. *Przemoc i poznanie: studium z nie-klasycznej socjologii wiedzy [Violence and Cognition: A Study on Non-classical Sociology of Knowledge].* Uniwersytet Mikołaja Kopernika: Toruń.

Court rulings

Court of Justice of the European Union

Joined Cases C-522/07 and C-65/08 *Dinter GmbH v Hauptzollamt Düsseldorf* and *Europol Frost-Food GmbH v Hauptzollamt Krefeld.*

Case C-142/06 *Olicom A/S v Skatteministeriet.*

Joined Cases C-362/07 and C-363/07 *Kip Europe SA and Others* and *Hewlett Packard International SARL v Administration des douanes – Direction générale des douanes et droits indirects.*

Case C-246/08 *Commission of the European Communities v Republic of Finland.*

Case C-197/09 RX-II *M v European Medicines Agency (EMEA).*

Case C-358/08 *Aventis Pasteur SA v OB.*

Case T-301/04 *Clearstream Banking AG and Clearstream International SA v Commission of the European Communities.*

Case C-52/09 *Konkurrensverket V TeliaSonera AB.*

Case C-449/08 *G. Elbertsen v Minister van Landbouw, Natuur en Voedselkwaliteit.*

Case C-109/88 *Handels- og Kontorfunktionærernes Forbund I Danmark v Dansk Arbejdsgiverforening, acting on behalf of Danfoss.*

Poland

Supreme Court of Poland

II CKN 465/98 wyrok SN 1999.09.16

Polish Constitutional Tribunal

(TK, SK 43/05) wyrok TK 2008.05.12 OTK-A 2008/4/57

Supreme Administrative Court

(NSA II SA 534/98) 1998.06.01 wyrok NSA II SA 534/98 LEX nr 41763,

(NSA II OSK 1287/06) Wyrok NSA W-wa 2007.10.02 LEX nr 394787

(NSA IV SA 1671/99) Wyrok z dnia 13 grudnia 1999 r. Naczelny Sąd Administracyjny (do 2003.12.31) w Warszawie IV SA 1671/99

(NSA IV SA 1671/99) Wyrok z dnia 13 grudnia 1999 r. Naczelny Sąd Administracyjny (do 2003.12.31) w Warszawie IV SA 1671/99

Courts of Appeal

(sad apel. I ACa 510/03,) wyrok s.apel. 2003.06.18 w Krakowie

(sad apel. II AKa 13/08,) Wyrok sądu apelacyjnego w Katowicach z dnia 15 maja 2008 roku, II AKa 13/08, LEX nr 447031, Biul.SAKa 2008/3/4, KZS 2008/9/41, KZS 2008/9/42

(sad apel. II AKa 13/08) Wyrok sądu apelacyjnego w Katowicach z dnia 15 maja 2008 roku, II AKa 13/08, LEX nr 447031, Biul.SAKa 2008/3/4, KZS 2008/9/41, KZS 2008/9/42

Voivodship Courts

(WSA I SA/Po 656/08) Postanowienie wsa w Poznaniu z dnia 21 października 2008 r II SA/Po 656/08 LEX nr 504611

(WSA II SA/Po 656/08) Postanowienie wsa w Poznaniu z dnia 21 października 2008 r II SA/Po 656/08 LEX nr 504611

(WSA III SA/Wa 2680/05) wyrok wsa 2005.12.30 w Warszawie

(WSA II SA/Łd 1086/02) wyrok wsa 2004.09.27 w Łodzi

(WSA III SA/Wa 542/09) w Warszawie wyrok wsa 2009.09.04

Part IV
Judiciary, Legitimacy, Democracy

Within Democracy's Reach? Revisiting Some Objections to Judge-made Law

Tilen Štajnpihler

Introduction

There is hardly any doubt that contemporary legal systems of the civil law tradition acknowledge the value and importance of case law. Numerous examples from courts and academia alike demonstrate the need to maintain a relatively stable and coherent judicial practise and emphasise that arguments derived from previous court decisions have a considerable justifying force in subsequent decision-making. This, in turn, implies that the judiciary plays a somewhat creative role in the functioning of a legal system.

Even consistent and long-standing judicial interpretations of statutory or constitutional provisions are, however, only to be understood as having *de facto* or persuasive authority and cannot constitute 'law' as such. Such a theoretical position can mostly be explained with regard to certain features of the historical development within the continental legal tradition and is sometimes justified by reference to compelling political and constitutional considerations. More precisely, the central question in this context is whether fully and openly recognising such an active role of the judiciary in the law-making process, which is implied by the growing importance of judicial precedents, can be reconciled with the *principle of separation of powers* and the closely related issue of *democratic legitimacy.*

The aim of this contribution is to explore these two fundamental concepts and doctrines of our constitutional and political order in this context and to raise some doubts about the claim that they provide a basis for a powerful objection to judge-made law.

The foundations of the objection

This well known objection is based on an 'age-old argument that legal change is the exclusive domain of the legislature, and that judges who have not been democratically elected and therefore lack the ability to make law with sufficient democratic legitimacy should refrain from doing so' (Haazen 2007, 13). This argument is a product of the legal and political theory of the times when the modern state began to take shape and it has been present ever since. Nowadays, however, this is not only a theoretical claim about how society should be governed, but a general attitude that has become an integral part of the civil law tradition. As one comparatist has put it, it reflects a kind of 'dominant folklore' about what judges do (Merryman 1996, 47).

Since Montesquieu many have argued in favour of establishing and maintaining a system of *separation of powers* to ensure democratic governance. In particular, the need to clearly distinguish and separate the legislature and the executive, on the one hand, and the judiciary, on the other, has been emphasised. The purpose of this organisational principle was not only to ensure independence for the judiciary, 'from the nature of its functions, [...] the least dangerous [department of power] to the political rights of the Constitution' (Hamilton, Madison, and Jay 2001, 382–383), as it usually has been stressed, but also to prevent intrusion of the 'judicial power, so terrible to mankind' (Montesquieu 2001, 175), into the areas – lawmaking and the execution of laws – reserved for the two other powers. As some have tried to show, historical abuses of power by the courts and the fear of the *government by judiciary* have shifted the continental understanding of the constitutional order into the direction of a strict separation of powers, rather than the system of checks and balances (Guarnieri and Pederzoli 2002, 137).

The flip side of this discussion concerns the question of judicial *legitimacy*. That state authority has to be justified with reference to democracy is almost commonplace in our society.

> The principle that coercion should be allowed only for the purpose of ensuring obedience to rules of just conduct approved by most, or at least by a majority, seems to be the essential condition for the absence of arbitrary power and therefore of freedom. (Hayek 1982, 5)

Based on the notion of popular sovereignty and the ideal of self-government, the principle of democracy provides a foundation for the legitimate exercise of state power. All state activity, especially law-making which imposes duties on citizens, must be directly or indirectly tied to the 'will of the people'. The weak majoritarian foundation of the judiciary is its inherent handicap compared to the political branches of the state. Therefore, judges should not be allowed to play a role in the law-making process and the effects of their decisions should be limited to the scope of the individual case. The following statement from the long-standing Slovenian minister of foreign affairs, made in an interview on 2 October 2011 in the magazine *Reporter*, can be considered as an ominous example of this 'sentiment':

> In particular recently decisions are being made in Slovenia by structures that hold a permanent office [i.e. have an unlimited term] and were elected by no one. I refer especially to the new businessmen, to tycoons, to bankers and also to *judges* [...]. The state must be governed by the parliament and the government or political parties that obtained their legitimacy for this purpose through elections. Affairs of state should not be regulated by people without authorisation!

Providing context and limiting the scope of the objection

By providing an explanatory context for this objection and pointing out what it usually refers to when it arises in the discussion of the proper understanding of the judicial role, we can considerably limit its impact on the notion of judicial law-making, especially in regard to the issue of judicial precedents.

Firstly, it is important to keep in mind that we are confronted with a theoretical dilemma: the objection challenges certain aspects of judicial activity at a level of political or constitutional theory. We are *not* primarily concerned with questions such as whether the courts are *suitable* – by the virtue of their design – to assume a more creative role in the law-making process or if they are *able* to carry it out effectively. Schauer, for example, pursues such a line of criticism when he talks about entrusting judges only with deciding cases and controversies:

> Although there might be strong arguments [...] that emerge out of any number of other values – separation of powers, democratic theory, the role of the courts, and the presumption against judicial review, for example, those arguments are not my focus here. Rather, my concern is with lawmaking *quality* and not with lawmaking *authority* [of the courts ...]. (Schauer 2006, 893)

The quality of judicial lawmaking is an important issue that concerns the practical aspect of judge-made law and challenges its ability to be an effective, systematic and therefore just instrument of social control. However, the objection at hand stays more or less at a theoretical level and argues that certain practices might not fit our political or legal order, simply because they are in conflict with some of the fundamental constitutional values. In short, we are not concerned about the *quality* of judicial lawmaking but about the question of its *legitimate authority*.

Secondly, the concerns regarding the separation of powers and democratic legitimacy were originally tied to the prevailing account of the nature of *law* and especially of *legal reasoning*. This is often illustrated with Montesquieu's famous characterisation of judges as being 'no more than the mouth that pronounces the words of the law' (Montesquieu 2001, 180). A similar view of what judges do when they are called to decide a case is also manifest in the so-called *declaratory theory of law* which for some time dominated the *common law* tradition (Cross and Harris 1991,

27–26). The basic idea behind this vision of law and legal reasoning is that in deciding a case the judge is always confronted with a body of fully developed pre-existing law which limits his creative power and appetite. Therefore, all that is expected of him is to *find* the law for the individual case without complementing or improving it in any way. In this context the separation of powers and legitimacy issues were – and to a large extent still are – connected to well known jurisprudential problems such as the 'open texture' of law and judicial discretion, the question of legal gaps and how they are to be properly remedied.

Related issues where concerns regarding the separation of powers and democratic legitimacy are being raised in connection to the role of the courts include *judicial activism*. If judicial activism is interpreted as an 'inclination to enlarge the power of the courts at the expense of the other branches of government' (Posner 2003, 211) and if one of the crucial arguments for the requirement for judicial self-restraint of a (constitutional) court 'is said to follow from its undemocratic structure' (Wright 1968, 9), it is not hard to comprehend why emphasising a more active role of the judiciary in the law-making process seems suspicious from the point of view of the established political and constitutional order.

The most notable discussion in this respect, however, revolves around the institution of the *judicial review of legislation*, placing constitutional adjudication in the spotlight. 'The competition between the Constitutional Court and the democratically legitimated legislature becomes acute primarily in the sphere of abstract judicial review,' writes Habermas, 'where the question whether a statute passed by parliament is constitutional [...] is submitted to judicial examination' (Habermas 1996, 241).

The discussion on the *judicial role* and the question of the *law-creating powers* of the judiciary, however, does not necessarily revolve around any of these issues – at least not directly. Our initial implication that the judiciary plays a more creative role in the functioning of a legal system as sometimes assumed and the claim that such a role should be openly recognised is not a contribution to the debate about, for example, judicial discretion or the limits of judicial review, where the objection regarding the separation of powers and democratic legitimacy most frequently arises. In fact, our interest is much narrower and concerns only the *significance of judicial precedent* for the understanding of the judicial role and the nature and legal status of court decisions. For the most part, we are only focusing on the implications of the fact that certain court decisions exert a *general legal* impact on future decision-making, i.e. their effect extends beyond the scope of the individual case. This fact can change our perspective of the judicial role.

Can judge-made law fit our constitutional design? (Re)interpreting constitutional and political doctrines

The objection against the notion of judge-made law, based on concerns regarding the separation of powers and democratic legitimacy, loses much of its force when applied to such a limited context. What remains is basically the 'insistence that the law is [or at least should be] made only by representative legislature', meaning that law – in its proper form – cannot be properly made, 'either directly or indirectly, by judges'. And if we take into account the requirement, 'that the judge may use only "the proper law" in deciding a case', this implies 'that he cannot base his decision on prior judicial decisions' (Merryman 1996, 36).

At the beginning it is useful to remind ourselves that judge-made law can hardly be considered a product of so-called *judicial legislation* (Barak 2006, 156). Judges making law by relying on the constraining effect of their decisions on future decision-making is clearly a somewhat different activity as when, for example, the body of representatives enacts a statute by majority vote in a legislative process. The judge does not enjoy the same 'liberties' as the legislator when setting a legal standard for the future, since the judicial process imposes different kinds of institutional restraints on him. For example, the courts themselves do not have the power to *initiate* the proceedings that would bring about legal change (Stone Sweet 2000, 140–141). Their range of possibilities is substantially limited by the factual context from which the individual case has sprung. The most important observation, however, is perhaps that the norms they put forward do not (usually) carry the same weight as general norms of the legislature. Judge-made law is subordinate to legislation: it must stay within its frame and can always be changed by it.[1] A good illustration of this relationship can be found in Kelsen's statement that 'the legislative function usually is distributed among several organs, but [...] only one of them is given the name "legislative" organ.' He continues: 'this organ never has a monopoly on the creation of norms, but at most a certain favoured position such as previously characterized' (Kelsen 2005, 272–273).

However, irrespective of these characterisations, some theoretical problems with interpreting the role and the status of judicial precedents and judge-made law remain. They are, it seems, tied to our conception of the *sources of law* (Lasser 2004, 169–174). It is in this context that issues of the separation of powers and democratic legitimacy re-emerge.

> In some legal systems and traditions, precedents are recognized only as pointers to interpreting codified law or law otherwise enshrined in statutes. This

1 We are leaving aside the institution of *judicial review of legislation* which, as mentioned above, opens up a range of issues concerning the relationship between the judiciary and the legislature.

> view depends on a strict understanding of the separation of powers as an element in sustaining the Rule of Law. Since the judges are not legislators, their decisions and opinions cannot be accepted as though they were themselves a source of law as distinct from being a persuasive guide to the proper interpretation of the law and laws made by the legislator. (MacCormick 2005, 144)

However, a number of qualifications can be made when interpreting these fundamental (legal) doctrines that seem to support the objection that case law violates the separation of powers and is inherently undemocratic.

Firstly, it is clearly not *conceptually* impossible to reconcile the idea of separation of powers with the operation of judicial precedent in a certain legal system (Barak 2006, 37–38). In fact, there are numerous jurisdictions that build on the same fundamental idea and have simultaneously incorporated the strictest formal doctrines of precedent, such as the English *stare decisis* had been at some point (Duxbury 2008, 53–57), without facing any serious opposition in the sense that it might be incompatible with the constitutional principle of separation of powers.

It is nonetheless true, as the Slovenian Constitutional Court has emphasised, that there exist several different implementations of the principle of separation of powers that correlate with the *specific historical* and *cultural* environment of individual constitutional systems (U-I-224/96, 05/22/1997, 16). Our constitutional doctrine of separation of powers never adhered to the strict version of this principle as it was originally conceived, but has always accepted the contemporary understanding according to which it is not possible to achieve a clear and sharp division of the main state functions, nor is that ultimately desirable, because it would go contrary to the very essence of this doctrine. Again, we can rely on the Constitutional Court, which has repeatedly stated:

> The essence of the constitutional provision dealing with the separation of powers is [...] in its fundamental function of protection of individual's freedom and dignity in relation to the government. Democratic efficiency of separation of powers, then, depends primarily on the quality of relations of mutual control, restriction as well as cooperation in the context of collective, balanced and efficient attainment of national objectives. (U-I-158/94, 03/09/1995, 20)

Clearly the court has put aside a purely formalistic interpretation of this constitutional principle and took a more purposive approach by emphasising the reason for limitations of state power in relation to the individual's fundamental rights. It seems that our current vision of the separation of powers is shaped by the *functional* approach as much as it has been traditionally construed by the *formal* approach to the organisational principles of state power.[2] Therefore the separation of powers is

2 Formalistic and functional approaches to the interpretation of the doctrine of separation of powers

best perceived as a kind of a *core functionalism* (Thomas 2005, 77). In short, it assumes that one branch can venture into the territory of another branch as long as it does not interfere with the core function of that branch. Therefore, each of the three branches has its core area of responsibility and the other two branches should refrain from any action that would disable that branch from *effectively* carrying out its *core responsibilities*. 'Structural differentiation, but overlap in functions are the norms' (Stone Sweet 2000, 130).

Interpreting the law is an integral part of the judicial function. The need for judicial interpretations of statutory or constitutional law to be consistent and stable can be explained and justified with reference to fundamental constitutional values tied to the rule of law (MacCormick and Summers 1997, 487–490). To provide for such a coherent body of judicial interpretations, some sort of mechanism of precedential constraint must exist – and indeed it does exist, called *jurisprudence constance* within the continental legal tradition (Fon and Parisi, 522–523). 'I am not concerned to inquire whether judges ought to be allowed to brew such a compound,' wrote Cardozo and continued, 'I take judge-made law as one of the existing realities of life' (Cardozo 2009, 10). If setting standards for consistent application of law in the future is a task that the judiciary already performs without any perceived threat to the separation of powers and if (certain) court decisions already exert a sort of constraint on future decision-making, then openly calling this activity judicial *law-making* and its product judge-made *law*, cannot be perceived as an unconstitutional intervention into the core of the legislative function.

Several adjustments can also be made when considering the requirements of *democratic legitimacy*. Firstly, the simple notion of *majoritarian democracy* has long been exposed as insufficient to cover all aspect of governing a contemporary political community:

> The traditional continental view that all power in a democracy must be derived directly from the popular sovereignty is generally rejected today on the grounds than all contemporary democracies are, in fact, *constitutional* democracies because they recognize that there are limits to what the majority can do. (Guarnieri and Pederzoli 2002, 159)

Emphasising *constitutional* democracy can hardly be considered a novelty; however, the notion still provides a good starting point which reminds us of the idea that democracy needs to be interpreted as being able also to sustain certain fundamental community values grounded in the constitution, such as the rule of law and human rights. As already mentioned, by using their interpretative powers and relying on their previous interpretations of the law, judges contribute to the 'sta-

---

are an important issue at the United States Supreme Court, 'where neither formalism nor functionalism has wholly dominated American constitutional history' (Eskridge 1998, 22).

bilization of normative expectations' (Luhmann 2004, 148) and thus serve some important values of the legal system.

Similarly, our understanding of democratic legitimacy must be sensitive to the central claim of different theories of *deliberative democracy* (Nino 1996, 121–134; Zurn 2009, 68–103) which highlight the fact that in some institutional contexts the simple aggregation of individual wills is not enough to justify certain community policies or laws. To fulfil the democratic requirement, law-making should entail the procedural deliberative component: 'decision-making by means of arguments offered by the participants to the participants who are committed to the values of rationality and impartiality' (Elster 1998, 8).

If we are prepared to concede that simple majoritarianism cannot be considered the sole foundation of democracy, other ways to justify the exercise of state power with reference to the democratic ideal become tenable. It no longer suffices to tie the notion of democratic legitimacy exclusively to the so-called *chain of legitimation* that runs uninterrupted from individual preferences to all political and legal decisions. 'Democratic pedigree' (Sunstein 1996, 46), i.e. democratic origin in their personal or organisational design, which the judiciary supposedly lacks, is not the only source of democratic legitimacy. Nowadays, a wide range of norms or criteria for assessing democratic legitimacy of governance practices are usually considered (Scharpf 1999, 17–28; Bekkers and Edwards 2007, 43–46; Wimmel 2009, 190–192).[3] Instead of looking only at the so-called *input* factors of democratic legitimacy, which are sometimes characterised by the slogan 'government *by* the people' and focus mostly on questions of participation and representation in the processes of law-making, we can turn to the so-called *throughput* and *output* factors of democratic legitimacy. These focus, firstly, on the characteristics of rules and procedures by which law is being made, and, secondly, on the result of these law-making procedures, i.e. on the substance of norms and decisions that state institutions produce. Here we are assessing, for example, whether the process of decision-making is *transparent* and can be identified as *reasoned deliberation* and whether it can be said that the decisions reached contribute *efficiently* to certain community goals, i.e. are *responsive* to community's interests and needs, and cohere with its fundamental values. In this context, democratic legitimacy is therefore sometimes labelled as 'government *for* the people'.

The variety of the conceptions of democratic legitimacy hinges at what was stated from the outset: our constitutional order has no problem accommodating a more *substantive* notion of democracy, as was implied even by the Slovenian Constitutional Court: 'The principle of democracy [...] in its substance and significance exceeds the definition of the state order as merely a *formal* democracy in which

[3] It should, however, be noted that these variables of legitimacy were primarily developed as a response to the problem of the democratic deficit of EU institutions.

laws and other regulations are adopted in accordance with the rule of the majority' (U-I-109/10, 09/26/2011, 10).

In addition, particularly when it comes to the judiciary, some argue that democratic legitimacy is best understood in connection to the notion of (democratic) *control* (Tschentscher 2006, 113–143). An institution is democratically legitimate if there exists at least a possibility of (direct or indirect) oversight or influence on the workings of the institution and its decisions by the community. Instead of focusing on the *organisational* or *personal* element as with the legislative body, where the means of control are mostly exhausted by the mechanism of periodical elections, the democratic control over the judiciary is centred around the *substantive* element, as the community is not necessarily involved in appointing the holders of power, but has an influence on the *content* of the decisions they make. This control can be exemplified foremost by the obvious feature of our constitutional design, i.e. that judges deciding cases and developing standards for future decision-making are bound by the constitution and statute law which provide a mandatory general legal framework for their activity that was created by the democratically 'unsuspicious' legislative body.[4] This *ex ante* control or substantive 'guidance' of the judiciary by the representative body is complemented by the permanent possibility of *ex post* control that has already been pointed out earlier: the permanent institutional ability of the legislature to change legal standards and doctrines established by judges and carried on by judicial precedents, designated as judge-made law.

Conclusion

Several studies have confirmed that the operation of judicial precedent is, in one institutional form or another, an integral part of contemporary legal systems (MacCormick and Summers 1997). It is an important factor that influences the creation and application of law in everyday practice. Fact is that judges *do* take prior decisions as grounds or reasons with which they justify their decisions. In this contribution we tried to demonstrate that the separation of powers and democracy alone cannot provide a sufficient reason to justify the claim that in doing so judges are neither making nor relying on *law* properly so called.

This position is, naturally, not free from theoretical difficulties. One of these is the inherent *retrospective* nature of case law. However, the objection based on its democratic illegitimacy and incompatibility with the doctrine of separation of powers is not among these difficulties. It can be dissolved if only we are prepared

4 There are of course other factors involved in the *substantive* or *content* dimension of (democratic) control closely connected to the judge's obligation to respect democratically enacted codified law, for example, the more sociologically grounded judicial professionalisation and legal indoctrination or, perhaps counter-intuitively, judicial independence. See Tschentscher 2006, 224–233.

to look beyond the traditional, plain-view interpretations of our political and constitutional concepts that can sometimes still be found in political rhetoric.

References

Barak, Aharon. 2006. *The Judge in a Democracy*. Princeton: Princeton University Press.

Bekkers, Victor, and Edwards, Arthur. 2007. Legitimacy and Democracy: A Conceptual Framework for Assessing Governance Practices. In *Governance and the Democratic Deficit: Assessing the Democratic Legitimacy of Governance Practices*, 35–60. Aldershot: Ashgate.

Cardozo, Benjamin N. 2009. *The Nature of The Judicial Process*. Cosimo Classics.

Cross, Rupert, and Harris, J. W. 1991. *Precedent in English Law*. 4th ed. Oxford: Oxford University Press.

Duxbury, Neil. 2008. *The Nature and Authority of Precedent*. Cambridge: Cambridge University Press.

Elster, Jon. 1998. Introduction. In *Deliberative Democracy*, edited by Jon Elster. Cambridge: Cambridge University Press.

Eskridge, William N. 1998. Relationships Between Formalism and Functionalism in Separation of Powers Cases. *Harvard Journal of Law & Public Policy* 22.1: 21–29.

Fon, Vincy, and Parisi, Francesco. 2006. Judicial Precedents in Civil Law Systems: A Dynamic Analysis. *International Review of Law and Economics* 26: 519–535.

Guarnieri, Carlo, and Pederzoli, Patrizia. 2002. *The Power of Judges: A Comparative Study of Courts and Democracy*. Edited by C. A. Thomas. Oxford, New York: Oxford University Press.

Haazen, O. A. 2007. Precedent in the Netherlands. *Electronic Journal of Comparative Law* 11.1: 1–21.

Habermas, Jürgen. 1996. *Between Facts and Norms: Contributions to a Discourse Theory of Law and Democracy*. Trans. by William Rehg. Cambridge: Polity Press.

Hamilton, Alexander, Madison, James, and Jay, John. 2001. *The Federalist*. Edited by George W. Carey and James McClellan. Indianapolis: Liberty Fund.

Hayek, F. A. 1982. *Law, Legislation and Liberty, Volume 3: The Political Order of a Free People*. London: Routledge.

Kelsen, Hans. 2005. *General Theory Of Law and State*. New Brunswick: Transaction Publishers.

Lasser, Mitchel de S.-O.-l'E. 2004. *Judicial Deliberations: A Comparative Analysis of Judicial Transparency and Legitimacy*. Oxford, New York: Oxford University Press.

Luhmann, Niklas. 2004. *Law As a Social System*. Edited by Fatima Kastner, Richard Nobles, David Schiff, and Rosamund Ziegert. Trans. by Klaus A. Ziegert. Oxford, New York: Oxford University Press.

MacCormick, Neil. 2005. *Rhetoric and the Rule of Law: A Theory of Legal Reasoning*. Oxford: Oxford University Press.

MacCormick, Neil, and Robert S. Summers, eds. 1997. *Interpreting Precedents: A Comparative Study*. Aldershot, etc.: Ashgate.

Merryman, John Henry. 1996. *The Civil Law Tradition: an Introduction to the Legal Systems of Western Europe and Latin America*. Stanford: Stanford University Press.

Montesquieu, Charles de Secondat, Baron de. 2001. *The Spirit of the Laws*. Trans. by Thomas Nugent. Kitchener: Batoche Books.

Nino, Carlos Santiago. 1996. *The Constitution of Deliberative Democracy*. New Haven, London: Yale University Press.

Posner, Richard A. 2003. *Law, Pragmatism, and Democracy*. Cambridge (MA), London: Harvard University Press.

Scharpf, Fritz W. 1999. *Regieren in Europa: Effektiv und demokratisch?* Frankfurt am Main, New York: Campus Verlag.

Schauer, Frederick. 2006. Do Cases Make Bad Law? *University of Chicago Law Review* 73: 883–918.

Stone Sweet, Alec. 2000. *Governing with Judges: Constitutional Politics in Europe*. Oxford, New York: Oxford University Press.

Sunstein, Cass R. 1996. *Legal Reasoning and Political Conflict*. Oxford, New York: Oxford University Press.

Thomas, E. W. 2005. *The Judicial Process: Realism, Pragmatism, Practical Reasoning and Principles*. Cambridge, New York: Cambridge University Press.

Tschentscher, Axel. 2006. *Demokratische Legitimation der dritten Gewalt*. Tübingen: Mohr Siebeck.

Wimmel, Andreas. 2009. Theorizing the Democratic Legitimacy of European Governance: a Labyrinth with No Exit? *European Integration* 31.2: 181–199.

Wright, James Skelly. 1968. The Role of the Supreme Court in a Democratic Society – Judicial Activism or Restraint? *Cornell Law Review* 54.1: 1–28.

Zurn, Christopher F. 2009. *Deliberative Democracy and the Institutions of Judicial Review*. Cambridge, New York: Cambridge University Press.

Cases

Slovenian Constitutional Court

U-I-224/96, 05/22/1997

U-I-109/10, 09/26/2011

A New Trend in the Debate on Justifying Judicial Review: Considering the Benefits of Judicial Reasoning

Ágnes Kovács

Introduction

In contemporary constitutional theory a great deal of theoretical attention has been devoted to the issue of justifying judicial review. Scholars have recently revisited the lively debate on the role of constitutional courts, which has resulted in a fundamental rethinking of the balance between judicial and legislative power at a more abstract level. Approaches denying courts the right to invalidate legislative acts and to have the final say on moral issues related to constitutional rights and principles have become more and more prevalent. As a result, the existence of constitutional courts is no longer self-evident. Opponents of constitutional review often claim that it is not the courts but the democratically elected legislature that should be entrusted with the power to determine the content of the constitution, and that, consequently, an institutional structure in which judges can have a special veto power over the decisions of the legislature, represents an unjustifiable distribution of political authority.

The heightened scepticism shown towards constitutional courts can be traced back to two main reasons. First, comments on judicial decisions mostly aim to address and evaluate controversial judgments and point out judicial errors, and this attitude gives the impression that the negative experiences related to the operation of US style constitutional courts are becoming more common.[1] Second, new forms of constitutional review have been institutionalised in Canada, New Zealand and

1 Mark Tushnet strongly criticises the performance of the US Supreme Court by citing numerous decisions from its practice to illustrate serious judicial mistakes. He states that the impacts of judicial decisions on political and public discourse are weak, and flawed judgments are particularly harmful to the protection of fundamental rights. Tushnet suggests that we should eliminate judicial review and return to the idea of popular sovereignty where constitutional issues are dealt with by the people (of the United States) through the ordinary channels of politics (Tushnet 1999, 154).

Great Britain, and this progress has become a robust stimulus for discussing judicial review as these new models have proven to be viable alternatives to the US model (Gardbaum 2010, 169).

Critics primarily address the so-called strong form of judicial review of the American kind, where courts have general authority to define the content of constitutional rights and invalidate legislative acts if they find them inconsistent with their own moral reading of the constitution. Since all political actors are bound by the justices' interpretation, which cannot be overruled in the original course of legislation, in the short or medium run the constitutional approach of the judiciary prevails. Consequently, it is not the legislature but a small intellectual elite who have the last word on what is demanded by political principles in a given situation. The US style judicial review is often considered an essential element of a new model of constitutionalism that has proliferated as a template over the past sixty years around the world. In academic commentary this 'new constitutionalism' – a regime of judicial supremacy – has been characterised by three distinctive features: (a) a written constitution with a catalogue of rights imposing constraints on the exercise of political power, (b) the higher legal status granted to constitutional rights by entrenching them against ordinary parliamentary voting, and (c) the establishment of judicial power for the enforcement of this higher status of the constitution by reviewing legislative enactments. Within this model effective protection of fundamental rights is basic to political legitimacy, and the judiciary plays the most prominent role in promoting rights protection (Sweet and Mathews 2008, 85–87).

One aspect of judicial supremacy is crucial for the aim of this paper. Namely, that the idea detailed above rests, at least in part, on the assumption that we are better off vesting the final power to decide basic constitutional dilemmas in the judiciary, since judicial decision-making is likely to provide better outcomes than the legislative process. So it seems obvious that when we deal with the institutional question and seek to defend the case we make for judicial review successfully, we cannot leave this assumption untouched. We need to address the way judges proceed in constitutional cases and take our findings about the character of judicial reasoning seriously. In this paper I aim to highlight the structural and defining features of judicial reasoning related to constitutional rights and to assess whether these features prove to be attractive for us to establish our claim for preserving a strong form of judicial review.

A procedural response to the institutional question

Before I turn to the examination of judicial decision-making, I briefly survey how the trend in addressing the issue of judicial review has developed in recent times. It may seem that Jeremy Waldron has played the most prominent role in this development if we examine how his claims have framed the discussion.

Theoretical efforts aiming to justify judicial review rely on two types of reasons: process-related and outcome-related reasons (Waldron 2006, 1372). Both concern the issue of the allocation of political authority but reach their conclusions in a different manner. Process-related arguments address the question whether a certain political procedure is in accord with our fundamental political principles, regardless of the outcome of that procedure. Outcome-related arguments, in contrast, settle the dispute on the basis of which institution is better positioned to reach a sound decision. That is, while process-related arguments contribute to the discourse through the concept of legitimacy, equality, participation or fairness, the question whether a procedure renders sound judgments depends mainly on the structural features of the institution concerned, and on the factors that characterise its reasoning. Debates about judicial review have primarily revolved around procedural considerations, and outcome-related arguments have so far received relatively little attention in this context.

Jeremy Waldron, who has elaborated a careful and celebrated account against judicial review on procedural grounds, for a long time seemed to neglect outcome-related reasons in the institutional debate. He suggested that we cannot decide whether judges or legislators are better at rendering sound judgments on constitutional rights issues because we disagree about what makes a judgment right or wrong, due to the lack of an epistemically reliable method of identifying objective moral truth. Although Waldron considered a consensus on the content of rights and on the theory of justice impossible, he regarded the fact of reasonable disagreement as a gain rather than an obstacle, a gain stemming from the concept of democracy itself. Disagreement reflects the fact that people take rights seriously. He argued that under the circumstances of politics, the community is divided by incommensurable and incompatible views about rights and justice, but a need is felt for common action to achieve the goals and values inherent in the political community (Waldron 1999, 101–103). Under these circumstances, since we are incapable of coming up with a theory of justice which every member of the community can agree upon, we have to establish fair procedures to create the basis for common action.

This is the reason why Waldron defends his case against judicial review on purely procedural grounds at the outset (Kavanagh 2003, 452). He claims that the idea of a strong form of judicial review in which judges are vested with the power even to strike down laws they consider unconstitutional is untenable in democratic terms, as judges lack the political legitimacy to settle the essential constitutional questions in the name of the community.[2]

2 Although the account Waldron advances is one in which the majority decision validates all legislative choices without any substantive limit, he does not exclude in principle all kinds of judicial

Waldron argues in favour of a constitutional arrangement in which disagreements about rights are settled by a legislative institution operating in a reasonably good order, on fair and regular elections, with universal adult suffrage and with responsible legislators who are accustomed to holding informed and sincere deliberation on issues of political morality.

This account entails that the majority decision necessarily privileges one conception among many other controversial conceptions as though the majority's decision were the community's own. The reason we should insist on the majority decision is that this is the only procedure which presumes a constrained sense of the notion of equal respect which can be grasped and endorsed by every citizen (Waldron 1999, 116). Equal respect in this impoverished sense means the commitment to give equal weight to each person's view. Conversely, for Waldron, any other plausible account of respect would be controversial and would privilege one individual's particular view of it, and thereby would fail to give equal weight to the other opposing views.

It is possible to draw a brief conclusion here and take a step towards the issue I am elaborating on in more detail below. The main reason Waldron advocates the legislative method of decision-making is that it proves to be the only mechanism which shows great respect for reasonable pluralism and the diversity of opinions by rendering collective judgments on basic moral issues without declaring one opinion right and the other wrong. The voting procedure does not entail the final settlement of disputes but leaves the discussion open for further consideration.

Furthermore, Waldron supposes that if we are incapable of reaching a consensus on basic moral questions and of convincing others of the truth of a moral statement, it is also impossible to decide whether judges or legislatures are better at approaching sound results. This entails that all accounts that rest on the consequences of decision-making processes fail and prove to be insufficient for an affirmative case for constitutional courts.

In view of the foregoing, it is probably surprising that in his recent works the focus of Waldron's attention has shifted from the procedural justification of judicial review to result-oriented considerations. He has carried out a circumstantial analysis of legislative and judicial decision-making in comparative terms and he seems to recognise that his approach against judicial review cannot be plausibly defended if he relies solely on procedural reasons and ignores outcome-related considerations. His procedural thesis that process-related reasons clearly argue in favour of the legislative method of resolving issues of justice is therefore complemented by

control over legislation. A weak form of judicial review is considered compatible with his account, i.e. 'a kind of institutionalization of the alertness to issues of rights', which allows judges to point out if significant issues of rights occur in the application of laws (Waldron 2006, 1370).

a result-driven approach. According to this, outcome-related reasons also support the preference for legislative processes.

Waldron seeks to challenge the supposition that judges are better at moral reasoning than courts in two steps. First, he indicates that judicial reasoning is occupied with, and distorted by, legalistic terms and doctrines which impede the invocation of genuine moral considerations when courts tackle serious moral questions. Second, in order to enhance the validity of his claim against judicial decision-making, he puts forward a normatively appealing account of the legislative method of resolving disputes.

I do not deal with the operation of the legislature here; instead I focus on the normative benefits of judicial decision-making. I will argue that Waldron misconceives the implications of adjudication on constitutional issues by courts.

Waldron's arguments against the judicial mode of moral reasoning

In laying out his argument on the defects of judicial reasoning, Waldron challenges some assumptions often claimed for courts, in order to establish the preference for the judicial method of reasoning (Waldron 2006, 1379-1386). The assumptions to which Waldron directs his arguments are the following: (1) judges encounter issues of fundamental rights in particular cases and not at the abstract level as legislators do. So they have to adjudicate on individual situations which offer them a better position to reason morally; (2) judicial reasoning is bound by the text of the constitution which ensures that judicial opinions are oriented towards the fundamental moral principles of the community; (3) the special burden of justification attached to judicial decisions requires judges to consider moral issues responsively and to reason in a careful way.

Waldron deems the previous assumptions confusing in many ways. He assumes that some give a false characterisation of the cases before courts, while others prove to be mistaken since the conditions involved in the assumption fail to improve the quality of judicial decisions.

As for (1), I agree with Waldron that the particular context within which judges address moral questions makes no difference to the point of reasoning they have to pursue. Both judges and legislators seek to discuss issues at a more abstract level, contrasting a wide range of reasons, even if the issue itself originated in an individual case. So neither institution can be considered better positioned to decide than the other. By contrast, I completely disagree with him that the constraints on judicial reasoning imposed by the text of the law (2) and the heightened burden to give reasons (3) would distract judges from its fundamentally moral character.

According to Waldron, judges are constrained by the political and institutional context in which they operate. Judges' main task is to find and apply general laws to individual cases and to determine the normative situations of those who come before the courts. Judicial reasoning is therefore compromised by legal texts, precedents and doctrines which make judges incapable of discussing the issue directly on its merits. The prevalent features of judicial reasoning are primarily determined by the functional and structural conditions of their work. Given these conditions, what judges engage in when they apply law is not moral reasoning in its ordinary and pure form but something quite different, which he characterises as a 'mélange of reasoning' (Waldron 2009, 12).

Waldron's argument also encompasses a relevant distinction between reasoning on one's own account and reasoning in the name of a whole society. He posits that the fact that public officials speak in the name of the whole community makes a difference to the character of their moral reasoning. Moral statements made by individuals stemming from an autonomous and responsible way of thinking aim to put forward moral principles on which individual actions and behaviours can be based and justified. Judges, by contrast, grapple with moral dilemmas related to a large number of individuals, so officials have to approach the issue in a way that illuminates what the community as a whole demands from its members in the cases concerned. This means that 'the officials in question have a responsibility to take seriously the views of others in a way that would not apply to individuals making moral decisions on their own account' (ibid., 15).

I think the distinction Waldron relies on is misleading and fails to grasp the common features that all kinds of moral reasoning ought to share. I argue that the status of the moral arbitrator does not change the nature and the aim of reasoning, although it imposes limits on the array of arguments that can be applied under the conditions of public debate.

Judges, like individuals, should be sensitive to the soundness and integrity of their reasoning. Both wish to appear responsible moral agents acting coherently out of respect for the truth. They would like to prove their willingness to test their convictions on more abstract considerations or even to alter or abandon their beliefs. 'So they try to explain their convictions in a way that displays reflection, sincerity, and coherence, even when they have no hope of converting others to those convictions' (Dworkin 1998, 1723).

Every responsible moral agent seeks to act on a coherent set of moral principles. And although judges are bound by the law in their reasoning, they are also tied to the fundamental principles of the legal system, and they should decide cases in the light of these basic principles even when they conflict with the text of the law. In constitutional matters it is more apparent that judges should appeal to controversial moral premises. The moral foundations of the legal system give way directly to more fundamental and deeper moral considerations that can be weighed by judges in the reasoning procedure. For example, if judges ought to rule on the constitutionality of laws mandating vaccinations for children, they should deal with the issue of parental autonomy and the question as to whether parents can be duty-bound to subject their children to interventions carrying potential risks for their health. This would entail further moral questions, e.g. the content of children's right to bodily integrity and their right to protection and care; to what extent parents can make decisions for their children in accord with their convictions and religious beliefs; the role of the state in protecting children's rights and the scope of the state's responsibility for protecting public health.

We can see then that judges are not insulated by law from engaging in a careful and honest moral reasoning, so judicial reasoning does not differ considerably from genuine moral reasoning. And we can conclude that Waldron's effort to contrast the moral reasoning of public officials to the reasoning of an individual is pointless.

The line of argument I have put forward so far indicates that even though the judicial process of resolving disputes requires, first and foremost, the application of the law and legal doctrine, it does not impair the fundamentally moral character of the debate on claims of constitutional rights. It seems we have managed to fend off the core challenge posed by Waldron to the judicial method of settling basic moral issues. Nevertheless, in order to complete our case for judicial review we should still set forth powerful reasons in favour of the judicial method of adjudicating constitutional rights.

The benefits of judicial decision-making in constitutional issues

Before elaborating on my claim for privileging judicial decision-making, I feel the need to disqualify two arguments which frequently appear in the debate as reasons for supporting judicial review.

(1) The idea that final authority over issues of constitutional rights should be delegated to judges instead of legislators does not imply that there is something specifically moral in argumentation about constitutional rights that requires moral capacities only judges own. I share the view that, ultimately, every authoritative action taken by public officials reflects a moral dilemma and it is, therefore, impossible to make public actions ignoring moral considerations (Sadurski 2009, 31). Even if we are contemplating whether a government should ask the International Monetary Fund for assistance in order to stabilise the country's financial situation or whether the issue is the extradition of a convicted murderer to his home country where his crime, motivated by ethnic hatred towards the victim, was glorified, we ultimately invoke moral principles to get at the heart of the dilemma. Whilst the

former case raises issues such as what is implied by sovereignty and to what extent the government should recognise its limited room for manoeuvre in issues of public finance, in the latter, we have to consider issues such as the general goals of criminal conviction, the importance of maintaining international peace, and the weight of the interest in preserving the country's good reputation within the international community.

This means that all public decisions, without exception, are fundamentally moral, so my efforts to justify judges' authority in having the final say in certain public issues do not rest on the special moral character of constitutional rights reasoning.

(2) Scholars like to emphasise that Waldron has directed his arguments against the thesis that judges are especially good at moral reasoning when compared to legislators (Fallon 2008, 1704). Although I do not share Waldron's conclusion in the institutional debate, I agree with him and his proponents that the thesis of judicial excellence formulated in this way is untenable. We cannot state in general that judges possess a special moral capacity that legislators do not. It would be a fallacy to assert that people in black robes are more prudent than other public officials and have special intellectual qualities that make them the most appropriate candidates to settle moral issues debated on behalf of the whole community. While they can acquire an appropriate range of experience during their tenure, this kind of moral routine is not something that other political actors or anyone engaging in moral reflection would lack. When John Rawls was concerned with the issue of defining a competent moral arbitrator, he insisted on describing a type of person who has common characteristics which ordinary people are able to possess. According to Rawls, a person with a certain degree of intelligence and knowledge, being reasonable and sympathetic to human interests relevant in the moral decision, and who disposes with an open mind to consider arguments and counter-arguments, is to be regarded as a competent moral judge capable of making serious moral choices (Rawls 1951, 178–180). All political actors can be portrayed by the characteristics Rawls attributes to moral judges. This shows that the distinction made between judges and legislators on their putatively different moral capacities is futile. Moreover, although public officials bear a great responsibility when they speak in the name of the community, there is nothing particularly unique, as I tried to indicate above, in the way judges address moral issues.

Regarding the shortcomings of the previous argumentation concerning the exclusive intellectual qualities of judges, we must establish a different argument which sheds light on the genuine virtues of judicial adjudication on fundamental moral questions.

Waldron is right in claiming that the range of the reasons that courts can legitimately appeal to is limited, but I think he misses the point when he considers this constraint as an obstacle rather than a gain in judicial reasoning. In a democracy political authority can only be legitimate if it is exercised by invoking reasons that all citizens can reasonably be expected to grasp and endorse independently of any wider, personal moral thinking. The reasons officials can have recourse to are public in the sense that they relate to the political community and to citizens generally; they express the idea of political justice applied to the basic structure of the society (Rawls 1993, 213). Public reasons are crucial for the principle of legitimacy. But how do public reasons impose constraints on public discussions?

The idea of public reason presents these constraints as a framework in which public deliberation can be conducted. This framework selects the arguments that authoritative agents can apply in justifying their acts. As a result, the burden of justification officials have to bear is heavy. Although both courts and legislatures are obliged to provide rational argumentation in accord with the requirement of public justification when imposing legal duties on individuals, there is a very significant difference between the two. The justification process plays a considerably more important part in judicial decisions than in legislative actions. Legislators may not need to adhere to publicly justifiable reasons so strictly since they can obscure any violation of the legitimacy condition by referring to the majority will. By contrast, the authority of the judiciary may be fatally damaged if it fails to meet the stringent criteria of public justification. It is thus not a coincidence – and reinforces the special burden of justification for the judiciary – that unlike legislative materials, the reasoning of a decision is a compulsory and inherent part of all judicial judgments. The merits of judicial review primarily stand in filtering out those reasons that carry weight in political discourse but prove illegitimate in terms of public justification (Kumm 2007, 19–20). Illegitimate reasons appearing in legislative processes can reflect prejudices, conventions and emotions, and these arguments often influence the outcomes of political processes. Courts have a serious responsibility in delineating the reasons on which legal acts can be based and it follows that they have the power to strengthen the general commitment of political actors to the idea of public justification.

Two examples drawn from the Hungarian judicial practice illustrate how courts can exercise control over political debates. Both verdicts show that the legislature has disregarded the limits of public justification and relied on considerations which turned out to be insufficient to justify the legal act concerned. In the first decision the Constitutional Court established that the law prohibiting a detained person from having access to legal counsel in the first 48 hours of the criminal procedure in certain cases violates the right to defence and to effective remedy.[3] The decision itself indicates that the government's argument, presented in the parliamentary debate, that some procedural guarantees can be set aside in order to prevent actions taken by the defendant or his or her lawyer in bad faith to obstruct or unduly delay

3 See the Decision of the Hungarian Constitutional Court 166/2011. (XII. 20.)

the procedure, proves unacceptable and illegitimate. This argument cannot justify restricting the defendant's rights, since it reflects the prejudice that suspected criminals tend to abuse the right to defence in order to deceive the authorities carrying out the investigation.

In the second judgment the Court declared that a local government law making rummaging in garbage cans illegal is unconstitutional as public peace and public order in general, or the comfort of residents, cannot be justified public reasons to restrict individual freedom.[4] This case demonstrates the law-maker's failure to entertain arguments which fulfil the idea of public justification, and provides an example how courts sweep away convictions and feelings, e.g. the aversion against the lifestyle of homeless people, from the decision-making process.

To conclude, if judges are authorised to override legislative acts, our representatives are forced to respect the limits of public reason, otherwise they can expect their decisions to be invalidated by the courts. This kind of judicial power imposes a heavy burden on legislators to act out of coherence and pursue their argumentation in a reasonable, disciplined and candid manner.

Furthermore, judicial control over legislation can improve the overall quality of public deliberation by informing the public about the constraints of public discussions that are likely to be ignored in favour of realising a policy-goal in the short run. Courts put a strong emphasis on specifying all the arguments and counter-arguments relevant in the debate and taking into account the total range of interests affected by the public choice. Judges analyse contested terms, assess arguments put forward by the applicants, consider reasons that justify the legislation, ask questions about the coherence of arguments and evaluate the consequences the relevant legislation implies. The practice of courts and their reasoning serves as a template both for political actors and for the public in general for how to engage in a reasoned debate about the content of political obligations. Citizens can notice the endeavour of courts to take individual rights seriously and to weigh the interests that are at stake in the debate. Hence, one point of having courts that are authorised to invalidate legislative acts is to provide a model of deliberation for the public and to offer guidance in structuring and conducting extensive public debates.

This is the reason I am inclined to advocate an institutional structure which respects judicial review as a guarantee to eliminate the defects in political processes. I claim that the special reason-giving character of courts has so much weight in the debate that it is advisable to authorise courts with a strong overriding power in the interpretation of the constitution.

4 See the Decision of the Hungarian Constitutional Court 176/2011. (XII. 29.)

Conclusion

In contemporary debates the issue of judicial review has mostly been addressed in procedural terms, and scholars have seemed to be reluctant to discuss the merits of judicial review on an outcome-related basis. Accordingly, I have presented a case for judicial review from a perspective which has so far remained without substantive theoretical reflection. In addition, what prompted me to focus on the nature of judicial reasoning is that recently, Jeremy Waldron has also appeared to attack judicial review from that angle.

In this paper, I did not state that, unlike legislators, judges have some special expertise to arbitrate in highly contested moral issues. Rather, it is the burden of justification put on judges that proves to be decisive in the debate concerning whose say should prevail in the cases dealing with constitutional essentials. I have argued that it is the judges who can ultimately define what reasons can be legitimately applied as public reason when justifying legal obligation. I also argued that it is the responsibility of the judges to prevent public deliberation from being eroded by non-public and partial arguments. This view is consistent with the Rawlsian conclusion that constitutional courts are the institutional exemplar of public reason. 'This means, first, that public reason is the sole reason the court exercises. It is the only branch of government that is visibly on its face the creature of that reason and of that reason alone' (Rawls 1993, 235). Besides, Rawls does not fail to emphasise that, as instances of public reason, constitutional courts fulfil a central educative role in public discussion as they give a reasoned interpretation of constitutional principles all citizens are expected to endorse. When pursuing this task, courts, indeed, make an important contribution to public debates held outside the courtroom: they push moral controversies to the fore and keep discussions alive without infecting them with illegitimate reasons. I claim that for this reason courts must be vested with the ultimate power to make decisions on significant constitutional matters.

Acknowledgement The publication is supported by the TÁMOP-4.2.2/B-10/1-2010-0024 project. The project is co-financed by the European Union and the European Social Fund.

References

Dworkin, Ronald. 1998. Darwin's New Bulldog. *Harvard Law Review* 111: 1718–1738.

Fallon, Richard H. 2008. The Core of an Uneasy Case for Judicial Review. *Harvard Law Review* 121: 1693–1736.

Gardbaum, Stephen. 2010. Reassessing the New Commonwealth Model of Constitutionalism. *International Journal of Constitutional Law* 8: 167–206.

Kavanagh, Aileen. 2003. Participation and Judicial Review: A Reply to Jeremy Waldron. *Law and Philosophy* 22: 451–486.

Kumm, Mattias. 2007. Institutionalizing Socratic Contestation: The Rationalist Human Rights Paradigm, Legitimate Authority and the Point of Judicial Review. *European Journal of Legal Studies* 1: 1–32.

Rawls, John. 1951. Outline of a Decision Procedure for Ethics. *The Philosophical Review* 60: 177–197.

Rawls, John. 1993. *Political Liberalism*. New York: Columbia University Press.

Sadurski, Wojciech. 2009. Rights and Moral Reasoning: An Unstated Assumption – a Comment on Jeremy Waldron's 'Judges as moral reasoners'. *International Journal of Constitutional Law* 7: 25–45.

Sweet, Alec Stone, and Mathews, Jud. 2008. Proportionality Balancing and Global Constitutionalism. *Columbia Journal of Transnational Law* 47: 72–164.

Tushnet, Mark. 1999. *Taking the Constitution Away from the Courts*. Princeton: Princeton University Press.

Waldron, Jeremy. 1999. *Law and Disagreement*. Oxford: Clarendon Press.

Waldron, Jeremy. 2006. The Core of the Case against Judicial Review. *Yale Law Journal* 115: 1346–1406.

Waldron, Jeremy. 2009. Judges as Moral Reasoners. *International Journal of Constitutional Law* 7: 2–24.

Cases

Hungarian Constitutional Court

Decision of the Hungarian Constitutional Court 166/2011. (XII. 20.)

Decision of the Hungarian Constitutional Court 176/2011. (XII. 29.)

Between Reflexivity and Effectiveness: Dilemmas of the Democratic Legitimacy of Constitutional Justice

Krzysztof J. Kaleta

Introduction

Research on the legitimacy of the contemporary public sphere poses many problems. These problems are related to the evolution of our understanding of the concept of power as such and the connected erosion of the current search for new formulas of its legitimacy. Although today power is no longer understood in terms of Weber's categories of domination (*Herrschaft*), and attention rather focuses on a communicative approach, the question of legitimacy is still an object of lively debate in contemporary legal and political philosophy. The issue of the legitimacy of power is even more important today because of the processes of globalisation and European integration which have remodelled its institutional form.

Being amorphous and dispersed, modern political power is difficult to control. However, without any criteria for assessment it is extremely difficult to verify its legitimacy in a reasonable way. We should remember that imposing normative constraints on power has always been the primary objective of constitutionalism. For this reason the theory of democratic legitimacy and the theory of constitutionalism are today inextricably linked.

In this paper I analyse the impact of institutional changes in the new constitutional order on the normative requirements (formulated in contemporary philosophical discourse) concerning legitimacy of constitutional judges. From a social science perspective legitimacy is perceived in terms of 'effectiveness' in human rights protection. It seems that such an approach needs to be complemented by the normative requirement of the 'reflexivity' of judges. However, the concept of reflexivity needs to be considered in two equally important dimensions: ethical and institutional.

Transformation of the public sphere and the concept of legitimacy

Contemporary political power is characterised by a strong institutional dispersion. As a result of this dispersion, areas of influence of particular branches of power overlap, including those of supranational character. This undermines the homogeneous approach to sovereignty. It also questions its manifestation, i.e. the general will. Today it is not as clear as it was hundred years ago that the will of the people expressed via universal suffrage gives a moral mandate to make decisions on behalf of the community. The general will expressed in the statute needs to be corrected by other institutional participants in the political and legal discourse. The dynamics of transformation of the public sphere means that the theory of separation of powers as proposed by Montesquieu has lost not only its descriptive character but also, according to some, its normative significance (Carolan 2009, 44–45). Consequently, we must consider how we can determine the foundation for the legitimacy of power in this new, changed form.

It is difficult to indicate a universal idea, based on certain values, which legitimises the new constitutional order in a complex way, in each of its institutional dimensions. This is because it seems that in contemporary social science the dominant way in which legitimacy is understood is not the search for a single and universal principle validating social order. It is rather treated as a complex process of communication, where arguments taken from various orders (moral, political, legal) can be made. The overlap of various discourses is one of the distinctive features of today's constitutionalism.

Despite the above-mentioned dynamic structural transformations, the claim that power requires legitimacy is still an axiom of modern political philosophy. Thus the arguments about the crisis of legitimacy of modern power in its different dimensions formulated more clearly among the public are the most important symptoms of the changes that arise in connection with the transition to new social structures: a new understanding of politics and constitutional institutions as tools for limiting them. Legal and political philosophers are beginning to recognise these processes, seeking appropriate analytical tools to explain their sources and determine a normative framework for these processes in relation to the constitutional institutions.

The difficulties of judicial supremacy: in search for a constitutional judge's legitimacy

It is clear that the judiciary, especially constitutional justice is the area of public administration which is growing most rapidly (Tate and Vallinder 1995; Hirlschl

2004; Whittington 2007). In this instance, the practice of adjudication has clearly overtaken theoretical reflection, which could provide tools for a critical analysis of judicial activity. The theory of democracy has long been searching for a formula to justify the competence of constitutional judges to strike down legislation directly legitimated in the process of universal suffrage, not only on the basis of legal constitutional principles, but also on the basis of strictly democratic principles by reference to such concepts as popular sovereignty or general will.

Ironically, in political systems constitutional courts perform the function of an institution legitimising the power of other political branches, primarily parliaments, by linking the current legislation with the law of a higher order, as expressed in the 'basic law'. Control of constitutionality, which intervenes far beyond the control of legality, is today a standard that should complement the legitimacy of the electoral legitimisation. The famous phrase contained in one of the French Constitutional Council decisions declaring that 'la loi votée n'exprime la volonté générale que dans le respect de la constitution' (the law expresses the general will only in so much as it conforms with the Constitution), has become the symbolic expression of the new democratic order.

This meant a final break with Rousseau's idea of representation. There is no doubt that the growing importance of constitutional courts is a reflection of the crisis of legitimacy of parliamentary bodies. The best evidence for this is the leading role of constitutional courts in the transition of political systems in Central and Eastern Europe where parliaments were weak, internally divided and unable to maintain a stable majority. The essence of this phenomenon is well captured by the 'invisible constitution', a term developed by the Hungarian Constitutional Court, or examples from Polish constitutional jurisprudence where judges derived a number of constitutional principles from the clause declaring the Republic of Poland 'a democratic state ruled by law and implementing the principles of social justice'. This liberal constitutionalism was based on mutually restrictive political and juridical elements. Therefore, the loss of confidence in politics and the limited liability of MPs has unavoidably resulted in an increase in the role of law in politics.

Contrary to Montesquieu's assertion that the power of judges is 'so to speak, invisible and null', the judiciary is playing an increasingly important role. It is even said that it is the twilight of the state of laws (*Gesetzesstaat*) and that a state of judges (*Richterstaat*) is being built out of the ruins. Hans Kelsen, the father of the continental model of constitutional justice, might think that the constitutional court is only one of the links in the system of technical and legal instruments of which the aim is to ensure compliance of the state's actions with the law. However, it seems that the modern role of constitutional courts is much greater. Nowadays it is difficult to recognise the constitutional judiciary as a single, sectoral link of the machinery of state. In fact, it has become a centre of policy-making in the state, the transformation of society, and in particular the legal position of the public at least as important as parliaments.

Constitutional courts play a key role in resolving the most important and most controversial issues of modern democratic societies. Politics has undergone what is called 'juridisation', which inevitably led to its judicialisation (Sweet 2000, 194–195). The increase in the role of legal rules in the functioning of community life means that intrinsically moral issues such as abortion, euthanasia or the death penalty, as well as strictly economic problems such as the pension or the health care system sooner or later come before the constitutional court.

Philosophers have tried to cope with the problem of legitimisation of constitutional courts in two ways. Thinkers who are sceptical of the role of courts in democracy are trying to reduce the role of judges to the function of arbitrators of separation of power. Judges should act to preserve respect for democratic procedures (Ely 1980, 87). These procedures allow proper articulation of the will of the people within the framework of traditional electoral institutions. On the other hand, the apologists of the authority of judges perceive them as depositees of the correct meaning of constitutional values and guardians of human rights (Dworkin 1986). Their task is to protect the sovereignty of individuals from the dangers posed by the majority. It seems that in contemporary constitutional practice doctrinal discourse is dominated by the latter justification. However, both formal and substantial approaches seem to be insufficient in taking into account transformations in the understanding of democracy and its legal framework determined by the ideas of constitutionalism. They are too static to respond to the challenges of the present day in the theory of democracy and constitutionalism in a satisfactory way.

The deliberative turn in the theory of democracy

It seems that in the last decades of the 20th century there was a significant deliberative turn in the theory of democracy (Dryzek 2000). Because of this turn, democratic legitimacy is beginning to be perceived in terms of the requirements of public deliberation on the collective decisions of the political community. In this way *isonomy*, the constitutive feature of democracy, is permanently linked with *isegoria*, the equal right to speak in a public debate. Basic principles of community life must be grounded in the consensus among rational, free and equal members of the public.

This trend is identified as a third way in political philosophy, overcoming the weakness of both constitutionalism based on Waldron's majority rule (Waldron 2001) as well as Dworkin's substantial constitutionalism focused on the protection of minorities. In the words of Ch. Zurn,

> Contemporary theories of deliberative democracy likewise attempt to combine a focus on the quality of decision-making process characteristic of expertocratic models with a focus on popular input and participation characteristic of populist models, without, however, succumbing to the potentially antiegalitarian elitism of the former or the potentially ungrounded decisionism of the latter. (Zurn 2007, 83)

Consequently, the distinguishing feature of contemporary theories of democracy is that the universal formulas of legitimacy which, by means of one general principle would comprehensively justify the institutional system are no longer applied. Modern concepts of legitimacy are rather pluralistic and argumentative in nature. Their aim is to integrate as much as possible the various participants in the democratic discourse by reference to the most widely accepted values which are more formal than substantial in nature.

Constitutionalism as good governance: towards output legitimacy and effectiveness

Referring to the second of the above mentioned research plans, it should be noted that nowadays we are dealing with an entirely new era in the history of constitutionalism. It seems that its main feature is the break with a strong opposition between legal and political components of constitutional order (Bellamy 2007). For this reason it is difficult to construct an adequate constitutional theory on the basis of the positivistic understanding of the constitution as a formal act capturing political life in the rigid framework of legality. The failure of the attempts to describe activist constitutional courts by the Kelsenian concept of a 'negative legislator' is the best evidence of this. For these reasons, as Eoin Carolan concludes, the constitution is 'a by-product of the practice of politics – purposive device whose true value lies in its instrumental efficacy rather than its ontological legitimacy' (Carolan 2009, 5).

One of the most visible trends in the transformation of modern constitutionalism is the dominance of the discourse on human rights in constitutional law. This is undoubtedly reflected in the increase in the importance of the constitutional courts. However, the dispute over fundamental rights is legal, political and moral at the same time. Therefore, judges isolated in a legal 'ivory tower' cannot fully participate in this debate. Legitimacy by reference to a specific value requires the right attitude. This interacts with the vision of an active lawyer in society more and more popular in legal culture. Adopting the perspective of those who are directly affected by the decision to be taken is required by moral considerations. This attitude can be interpreted as a form of political representation.

As a consequence, the concept of the legislator takes on a new pluralistic meaning. Legislation itself has become a collective enterprise, a result of the synergic acts of all the participants in the legislative discourse. At the same time a significant feature of modern constitutionalism is the emphasis on the 'effectiveness' of constitutional institutions, which in relation to courts means first and foremost the effective protection of fundamental rights of the individual.

This effectiveness can be interpreted in two ways. On the one hand, it can be seen as an attempt at professionalisation on the part of judges who see themselves as guardians of fundamental rights which are legally conceptualised and have objectified substantial content. On the other hand, it can be seen as compliance of settlements with the will of the people recognised more in terms of empirical categories. The first model corresponds to the traditional scheme of constitutional institutions understood as instruments of self-limitation of the people's power in the name of protection of private autonomy of the individuals. The second one is closer to popular constitutionalism, perceiving constitutional institutions as forums for the realisation of public autonomy of the members of the political community (Tushnet 1999; Kramer 2004).

Thinking about the changes in the understanding of the role of constitutional courts in the theory of democracy and the rule of law requires us to contemplate new forms of control of judges that would be adequate to meet the new challenges. It seems that in this context it is possible to distinguish two independent approaches to the control mechanisms and legitimacy. Taking constitutional courts as a reference point, they may be described as control oriented at external and internal legitimacy, respectively. The former focuses on justification towards the people; in the latter, legitimacy is kept within the legal practice in which judges are directly involved. To some extent, these approaches correspond to the two types of effectiveness referred to above.

There is a necessary tension between the awareness of the public on the one hand and the focus on effectiveness of exercising of power (*output legitimacy*) on the other. Consequently, the importance of responsiveness and reflexivity in judicial work increases. Judges are treated as participants in public deliberation, yet they are involved both in general practical discourse as well as in the legal discourse which is a special kind of the first. It seems that among these new circumstances, courts may legitimise their power primarily through effectiveness in the development of a reflective framework of human rights discourse. 'Constitutional politics' practiced by judges in order to keep their legitimacy should be characterised by a clear intensification of public deliberation, understood as an important factor of democratic control. It must not be forgotten that the original purpose of constitutionalism was to make democracy controllable.

It seems that these processes are aptly described by the concept devised by Robert Alexy who, in his *Theory of Constitutional Rights* (2002), has attempted to overcome the problem of the multiplicity of possible interpretations of constitutional provisions which may occur through such a discourse. According to Alexy, moral theory has to be combined with a theory of law. The German philosopher distinguishes four so-called stages of the system of law: general practical discourse, legislative procedure, legal discourse and court procedure. General practical discourse, subordinated to the requirements of practical reason, does not lead to 'one right answer'. Meanwhile, social practice requires a specific solution. The institutionalised law-making procedure resulting in the settlement of the legislature serves this purpose. However, a law adopted in this way will not be able to resolve all possible cases within its textual framework. That is why the third stage, namely legal discourse, is necessary. Although it is not institutionalised, it is already limited by legal culture: laws, precedents, and doctrine. Because of these restrictions, the uncertainty of the result is much reduced, although not completely eliminated. Hence, there is need for the emergence of the next phase of the process, which is of an institutional and decision-making character at the same time. Since the parliament cannot act on its own, the intervention of a constitutional court becomes necessary (Alexy 2002, 369–371). A decision reached in this way gains both discursive rationality and decisiveness necessary from a functional point of view. This vision of constitutional adjudication is consistent with deliberative models of democracy, while at the same it assigns them a more efficient character. In this way, constitutional institutions, traditionally focused on the effectiveness of legally conceptualised fundamental rights, must somehow establish communications with the public sphere to enhance their legitimacy. Case law should reflect the dynamics of social changes within the meaning of constitutional values, taking into account the horizontal dimension of fundamental rights.

Reflexivity as the missing link

Because of the circumstances outlined above, reflexivity grows into a core value of the new constitutional order. As I mentioned above, for constitutional courts *de facto* legitimacy is perceived in term of effectiveness in human rights protection. Whereas reflexivity is a fundamental normative requirement addressed to constitutional judges, its role is to ensure *de iure* legitimacy.

The new significance of the idea of reflexivity was most fully expressed in the works of Pierre Rosanvallon, who identified 'reflexivity' as a central value legitimising the power of constitutional judges. Not giving up on the classic democratic vocabulary such as sovereignty of the people or the general will, the French philosopher points at a triad of values: impartiality, reflexivity, and proximity. These values respectively determine the source of legitimacy of modern authority in relation to the individual bodies exercising it.

Reflexivity is to be manifested in the judges' efforts to make a broad spectrum of individual perspectives, that make up the constitutional identity of the polity, 'present' in the constitutional discourse of the community (Rosanvallon 2008, 195–196). In this way, and not only by deficient electoral procedures or juridical axioms, the principle of popular sovereignty is to be realised through the constitutional institutions. With such a set of criteria the appointment process of constitutional judges becomes a secondary issue. It is the ethical qualities and substantive qualifications of judges that count when assessing their legitimacy.

The reflexive authority has to stimulate the process of political empowerment of individuals. The role of a constitutional court therefore is to create conditions for the full expression of the identity of citizens in the public sphere. Reflexivity understood in this way indicates a radical break with the existing paradigm of constitutional judiciary and with the vision of the judge perceived only as *la bouche de la loi*. It also means granting the judiciary the right, on equal footing with the parliament, to speak 'on behalf of the people'. Thus, the general will is dispersed, finding its expression in various institutional forms. However, constitutional courts would not represent voters but 'the people' as a symbol constituting the figuration of those political principles which express the ethical foundation of society. Its elements would be in particular equality, the pursuit of legal inclusion of any diversity, and respect for fundamental rights in the public domain. According to Rosanvallon, the appropriate democratic architecture should be founded on two institutional pillars: the parliament channelling social conflicts and the constitutional court as the centre of integration and support for consensus on the grounds of the basic constitutional principles.

Such an understanding of the reflexivity of judges means a radical break with the traditional liberal paradigm of constitutional judiciary. First of all, this approach questions the division of constitutional instruments into legal and political ones. In light of liberal constitutional theory, the former imposed objective limits on the realisation of current politics. Consequently, with this new approach, the non-political character which has traditionally been raised as an argument in support of the legitimacy of this institution is questioned.

The constitution itself also gains a new status. As mentioned above, in the theory of liberal constitutionalism the constitution was an instrument of society's self-restraint. In the context of Rosanvallon's theory, the impossibility of a firm and final self-determination of democratic community means the abandonment of the traditional idea of liberal constitution in favour of moral and political principles which are abstract and not rooted in the text of the constitution, but formed in spontaneous discourse (Rosanvallon 2008, 213). Thus, the role of constitutional courts in a democracy is to moderate constitutional discourse, to ensure openness and equality of the process of deliberation. In Rosanvallon's words, one of the functions of the modern state is 'not only to reflect society *as it is* but also to contribute to society's reflection on itself so as to assist in the formation of a true collective consciousness' (ibid., 336). This task is to be fulfilled by the constitutional judiciary which, in order to remain a reflective power should focus its immediate attention on the individual anew.

The degree of legitimacy of constitutional courts is thus determined by a judge's effectiveness in influencing constitutional practice, but influence is understood more widely than in the traditional way, i.e. as part of the implementation of the principle of good public governance. It is therefore an authoritative settlement of the kind which will ensure the empowerment of the people to the maximum possible extent, by treating them as stakeholders and not just as passive representatives of a collective titular sovereign. The concept of reflexivity is proposed by the French philosopher as a response to the faint and almost non-existent participation of the public in the exercise of judicial power in modern political systems.

Two dimensions of reflexivity

Within this vision, constitutional courts play an important role in shaping the constitutional identity of the political community. This makes it easy to abuse power. These institutions can adopt the role of 'social engineering centres'. This would mean constitutionalism without a constitution and a return to the Platonic idea of philosopher kings and would have nothing in common with democracy. Therefore, in my view, the legitimisation formula adopted by Rosanvallon can only be maintained if there exist a strong civic sphere and an institutional architecture designed in a dialogical way. This requires to develop an appropriate model of institutional communication between judges and the public as well as other instruments to ensure synergy between activities of the constitutional court and the Parliament, so that combining their relationship is not just a relationship between the controlling and controlled but the process of reaching the optimal policy decisions. These problems concern political and legal culture.

In fact, the new model of legitimacy can be maintained only provided the courts do not speak in the name of the people, but allow them to speak freely, while ensuring equal access to public deliberation. Reflectivity would then occur primarily due to judges' concern for the openness of channels of communication. Here it will be important to protect the fundamental freedoms of communication such as freedom of speech or access to public information. However, it will also be important to make the constitutional court an institution deliberating both from the inside (through consensus-oriented procedures of judicial decisions) and in its relations with social networks to be defined as 'allies of the court' (*amici curiae*). They would provide an 'information flow' to the court in dealing with complex issues that require capturing a number of dependencies which are difficult to deal with at the stage of abstract control (in the horisontal interactions of fundamental rights), thus revealing the complex structure of the network society.

The growing importance of communication between the constitutional court and the public exposes the question of institutions that serve as bridges between the practice of case-law and social practice. This function can be performed by the reflexive justification of a court, the aim of which is to take into account any relevant arguments and to convince the public as to the fairness of the decisions. Reflexivity does not signify a reduction of the field of analysis to the narrow perspective of expertise, such as juristic expertise; rather it means the interpenetration of different outlooks and in consequence the transformation of particular opinions. For this, hybrid forums are needed where the academics meet the public. Only on the basis of this assumption can the system of knowledge co-legitimise the institutional sphere on a par with the electoral process.

Ultimately, however, one needs to be aware that reflexivity as an active approach accompanying the exercise of power also has an ethical dimension. At this level the most important factor seems to be the determination of the deontological and ethical obligations ensuring judicial self-restraint. Reflexivity requires an ethical foundation to protect against the danger of the general will being replaced by the personal views of judges. Without a judge's impartiality, a 'state of reflective equilibrium' in the legal constitutional discourse cannot be guaranteed.

As noted by J. M. Maravall, experience demonstrates that democratic ideology can be used to disavow the legal framework and the role of judges in public life, and the judicial system can be a tool for dismantling the democratic rules of the game (Maravall 2003, 274–275). Modern democracy is looking for instruments that would reopen those orders at each other without the essence of any of them being affected. Hence the search for a forum that would allow people to speak effectively within the 'empire of law' without disrupting the stability of the constitutional order. A forum of this type may be a constitutional court but only on the condition that its institutional shape is properly designed. It should provide judges with tools to maintain a reflexive constitutional framework for a dialogue among institutions and between institutions and society.

Note This paper is an expanded version of an article which appeared in Polish under the title: Sądownictwo konstytucyjne w warunkach ponowoczesności [Constitutional justice in the era of post-modernity] in *Teoria prawa między nowoczesnością a ponowoczesnością [Theory of law between modernity and post-modernity]*, ed. A. Samonek. Kraków: Wydawnictwo Uniwersytetu Jagiellonskiego, 2013.

References

Alexy, Robert. 2002. *A Theory of Constitutional Rights.* Oxford: Oxford University Press.

Bellamy, Richard. 2007. *Political Constitutionalism.* Cambridge: Cambridge University Press.

Carolan, Eoin. 2009. *The New Separation of Powers. A Theory for the Modern State,* Oxford: Oxford University Press.

Dworkin, Ronald. 1986. *Law's Empire.* Cambridge (MA): Harvard University Press.

Ely, John. 1980. *Democracy and Distrust.* Cambridge (MA): Harvard University Press.

Hirschl, Ran. 2004. *Toward Juristocracy: The Origins and Consequences of the New Constitutionalism.* Cambridge (MA): Harvard University Press.

Kramer, Larry D. 2004. *The People Themselves: Popular Constitutionalism and Judicial Review.* New York: Oxford University Press.

Maravall, José María. 2003. The Rule of Law as a Political Weapon. In *Democracy and the Rule of Law,* edited by José María Maravall and Adam Przeworski, 261–301. Cambridge: Cambridge University Press.

Rosanvallon, Pierre. 2008. *La légitimité démocratique. Impartialité, réflexivité, proximité,* Paris: Seuil.

Stone Sweet, Alec. 2000. *Governing with Judges: Constitutional Politics in Europe.* New York: Oxford University Press.

Tate, C. Neil, and Vallinder, Torbjörn. eds. 1995. *The Global Expansion of Judicial Power.* New York University Press.

Tushnet, Mark. 1999. *Taking the Constitution away from the Courts.* Princeton: Princeton University Press.

Waldron, Jeremy. 2001. *Law and Disagreement.* New York: Oxford University Press.

Whittington, Keith E. 2007. *Political Foundations of Judicial Supremacy.* Princeton: Princeton University Press.

Zurn, Christopher F. 2007. *Deliberative Democracy and the Institutions of Judicial Review.* New York: Cambridge University Press.

Part V
The Boundaries of Criminal Justice

Shielding Criminal Justice from Politics

Mojca M. Plesničar

Introduction

The '(re-)insulation' of criminal justice policy-making is a proposition that has been suggested by several criminologists and other commentators of recent developments in the field of criminal justice (Pettit 2002; Zimring and Johnson 2006; Lacey 2007; Sherman 2009). The common underlying assumption of such suggestions is an explicit denouncement of the *status quo*, in which the field seems to have been taken to intolerable levels of politicisation, in turn producing overly punitive policies and practices. While the advocates of the return to a state where crime is insulated from the openly public and political debate seem to believe that this is a feasible and indispensable measure, the considerations to be made in determining the final answer are many.

In this paper, I will first briefly outline the reasoning of different proponents of insulation in criminal justice policy-making and their arguments for such an approach. I will then consider whether the solutions they put forward bring about desirable outcomes for modern societies and examine some potential drawbacks. I will finish the discussion with some general remarks on what (re)insulation would mean and whether it is at this time a desirable and possible aim.

Direct public involvement as a generator of punitiveness

The proponents of the 'insulation model' (Loader 2009, 6) together with many others involved with criminal justice seem to agree that current trends in criminal justice are illiberal, unwise and detrimental to modern societies as a result of the field's increasing entanglement with politics. The notion of politicisation implies first, an invasion of the criminal justice field by political, typically electoral considerations shaping crime policy (Lacey 2007), and second, an escalating exposure of criminal justice issues to the public and especially the media, producing initiatives and proposals for further changes in criminal justice. It seems to be a shared view that the consequences of the augmented public involvement with criminal justice policies combined with a declining trust in professionals in the field cannot but produce non-systematic, largely ineffective and, most importantly, extremely harsh policy outcomes (Pettit 2002; Zimring et al. 2003; Lacey 2007; Sherman 2009).

However, the trends in the US and the UK criminal justice systems which seem to be the main issue causing concern and calling for 'insulation' from politics, can hardly be acknowledged 'elsewhere' (Albrecht 2001, 294). Accounts by such authors as Garland (2001) and Simon (2007) that paint a discouraging picture about the present and likely future of criminal justice in those countries cannot be easily transplanted to e.g. Scandinavian or many other continental European countries (Albrecht 2001; Tonry 2004; Nelken 2009). Still, some similarities cannot be ignored. Even though imprisonment rates or other punitiveness variables differ strikingly among European countries, they do not always correspond to the levels of criminal justice politicisation in the respective systems. While it can be rather safely said that the level of politicisation in neo-liberal states (Cavadino and Dignan 2006) or liberal market economies (Lacey 2007) by far exceeds the levels in other countries which are more moderate in terms of punitiveness, even such leniency hallmarks as Sweden are not immune to the politicisation of criminal justice (Tham 2001), much less so Central and Eastern European countries which are in the middle range of the punitiveness spectrum. The 'heating up' (Loader and Sparks 2010) of criminal justice is therefore not an exclusive feature of the 'neo-liberal' states, but rather a pervasive aspect of many modern societies. The seemingly linear correlation between politicisation and increased public involvement with criminal justice on the one hand and punitiveness on the other might be less clear than it seems.

In recent years there has been extensive debate on the reasons and processes that have produced the harsher reality criminal justice systems have become entrenched with. Accounts of the changing dimensions of society in 'late modernity' influencing criminal justice (Garland 2001) can be sided by narratives of deliberate 'top-down' changes to criminal justice rooted in alternative motives (Wacquant 2009; Simon 2007). Others have proposed explanations in terms of different cultural backdrops (Whitman 2005), political economy systems (Cavadino and Dignan 2006) or electoral systems (Lacey 2007). While the real reason or combination of reasons for the changes and differences in their complexity may remain unclear, by looking for a range of factors, both comparatively and historically, bearing in mind that the variables may differ through time and space, while also taking into account the 'larger picture' of social and not merely institutional harshness, by time we can get clearer answers (Tonry 2007; Nelken 2006).

In the meantime, the reality of criminal justice causes unease for many modern day criminologists. The solution that the proponents of insulation offer is to remove the formation of criminal-justice policies from the heated environment of politics and shelter it to a smaller professional setting which would be suitable to make conscious, rational decisions without public interference.

The reasons they offer for such a proposition are numerous and different. Pettit explains the need for such a change applying MacDonagh's 'Outrage Dynamic' to criminal justice. He describes three preconditions for an outrage spiral – the exposure to an evil, popular outrage as a result of the exposure, and a due reaction to the outrage by the government – which fit rather nicely with current occurrences in criminal justice policies. Pettit's conclusion which finally leads him to a plea for a different, isolated policy-making system, is that 'wherever the outrage dynamic can get a grip, it will tend to drive sentences [...] towards the cultural maximum' (Pettit 2002, 437).

Pettit claims that because such policies are created as exceptional cases come along, there can be no system, no premeditation, and no rationality in them. The only driver of such policies is the gratification of a public desire for (re)action, resulting in non-systematic, at times even contradictory policies. Moreover, what is perchance most disquieting for a democratically oriented reader of Pettit's work, is that in his account democracy which is so highly regarded by modern societies is the very root of the problem.

> [T]here is something about democracies that militates against reasoned policy-making. [...] [T]he society is democratically organized in such a way that politicians are going to be required, on pain of electoral sanction, to respond in a more or less persuasive way to the outrage. [...] They will have to react to the popular outrage by showing themselves to be at least as outraged as the general run of people – and to be determined, with resources at their disposal, to do something about it. (Ibid., 429, 433, 435)

Like Pettit, Lacey (2007) believes that insulating the policy-making process from public exposure is the way out of excessive harshness. She also offers two additional arguments for such an approach. First, she claims that not only is current crime policy at odds with reason and liberal values, it is also something that very few would wilfully choose to pursue if all the consequences, mainly the 'increasing social polarisation', were weighted at its creation: 'Unmediated penal populism leads [...] to a world for which perhaps few, even among the relatively advantaged, would consciously choose to vote' (Lacey 2007, 185).

At this point it may be useful to recall Herbert Simon's famous work on 'bounded rationality' as applied to the political decision-making process. When public demands, informed by extraordinary examples and limited information, are met by politicians without hesitation for fear of political (electoral) loss, the resulting policies have no chance of encompassing all important considerations, for the sole reason that they were not available or pondered by the public at the decision-making stage (Fischer 2005). The voters' preferences, as rational as they seem within their 'bounded' framework, may result in unsuccessful if not counterproductive decisions no one would knowingly opt for.

As a second argument, Lacey introduces the economic dimension of modern governance. After discussing Freeman's analysis on the intersections between crime and economy she comes to the conclusion that since 'high rates of imprisonment make only a modest difference to crime levels [...] it seems sheer economic irresponsibility to invest an ever-growing proportion of GDP in the prison budget' (Lacey 2007, 189).

Insulating criminal justice policy-making would thus, according to Lacey, not only produce policies that are more in line with the 'real' preferences of the voters, but it would also take into account cost-benefit analyses, encompassing the economic as well as the social costs of the proposed measures.

Direct democracy is also portrayed as problematic by Zimring and Johnson (2006), who develop their theory through the example of the Californian criminal justice system (Zimring et al. 2003). They take citizens' hostility towards criminals as given, i.e. as a 'chronic condition' which is necessarily reflected in democratic societies. According to the authors, one of the main reasons why not all democracies across the globe implement ever harsher policies is the professionalisation of the policy-making process, i.e. its removal from direct democratic control. This 'leniency vector' supposedly filters 'innate' public demands for harsher punishment and is able to produce more rational (in the sense of less punitive) policies.

Another call for rationality in the policy-making process comes from the field of experimental criminology. Sherman (2009) laments the fact that there is so little room for evidence in current criminal justice policy-making process. Proposing a more systematic approach he gives two possible solutions, the 'bottom-up discretion' model, where evidence on the effectiveness of individual measures is presented to and taken into account by decision-makers in individual cases, and second, the 'top-down guidance' model, the one he favours. Here committees of professionals develop policy guidance based on systematic reviews of evidence, all of which would be monitored and directed by an independent evidence-assessment agency. As a result Sherman believes that crime policy would become more rational and its rooting in evidence would allow for the elimination of non-effective, purely expressive measures.

The benefits of shielding

By agreeing that democracy as it actually operates in modern societies is part of the problem the proponents of insulation exhibit something that might well be described as a 'Platonic fear of democracy in the field of crime and punishment' (Loader 2009), and they seek to limit its negative effects by putting some restraints on the democratic process itself (Lacey 2007; Zimring and Johnson 2006; Pettit 2002). In so doing they need to explain what exactly it is that makes criminal justice so different from other fields of governance that would justify such an approach.

Some have resorted to an analogy with the field of economics, where monetary policy and especially the setting of interest rates has been removed from the hands of politicians and delegated to independent central banks, which are better able to make informed and cautious decisions and avoid harmful ones taken in the heat of political considerations (Lacey 2007; Zimring et al. 2003; Pettit 2002). Since politicians are unable to resist public insistence on harsher policies, they should remove themselves from the equation completely (Pettit 2002).

The suggestion that criminal justice is a field with distinguishing characteristics which calls for a different treatment is not new. For instance, Rawls (1993) has maintained that questions of criminal justice are inadequate for public debate and politics because they excite the public sentiment too much to allow for good governance.

The field of criminal justice may also be viewed in terms of the majority – minority relationship, a question that has been present since the early days of modern democracies (Tocqueville 2003). When the majority (the public) has the ultimate power to decide on the fate of the minority (the offenders), among the mechanisms mitigating the 'tyranny of the majority', Tocqueville finds one that is strikingly similar to what the proponents of insulation seek to portray:

> [T]he authority they have entrusted to members of the legal profession, and the influence which these individuals exercise in the Government, is the most powerful existing security against the excesses of democracy. (Tocqueville 2003, 216)

For Tocqueville the powers entrusted to this new 'American aristocracy' – the members of the legal profession, who are allowed to take crucial decisions without reference to majority views, are the safeguard for democracy not going 'too far'. While the insulation model does not limit the set of professional bodies to which policy-making in criminal justice would be designated to, only to the legal profession, there is a similar logic in keeping the public (or the majority) out of the crucial decision-making processes. Again, the notion that too much public involvement (too much democracy) would have harmful consequences for society is clearly present.

At a more pragmatic level, the proponents of insulation offer a range of arguments as to why the shift to the new model is indispensable. Firstly, the leniency in punishment exhibited in systems where criminal justice has been left mostly to the hands of professionals, as compared to the harshness in system where such a practice has been discontinued, could in itself be enough to persuade a more liberally oriented reader (Tonry 2004; Zimring et al. 2003). If we understand excessive harshness in punishment as detrimental and agree on the fact that in neo-liberal states the 'healthy' levels of harshness have been surpassed, then any way of reducing the disproportionate severity to a more moderate level should seem worthy of consideration.

Secondly, at present policies in criminal justice are often constructed as responses to the public outrage in exceptional cases capable of stirring public emotion (e.g. Megan's Law in the US, the Bulger case in the UK, Marija's Law in Serbia, etc.). Combined with the increased power of the victims' rights movement this draws dangerously close to what Montesquieu famously warned against: 'On the pretext of avenging the republic [the victims?], one would establish the tyranny of the avengers' (Montesquieu 1989, 203).

The proposed insulation model would safeguard policy-making from hastened reactions to such initiatives and allow for a systematic and considered decision-making process (Pettit 2002). Moreover, if the shielded professional body was to accept Sherman's argument for an evidence-based approach, the produced policies could have a firmer grounding in empirical data on what has been proven successful and what not. It would also allow for the elimination or at least the limitation of policies which only serve symbolic, punitive purposes and are unsuccessful in other aspects, mainly in reducing recidivism (Sherman 2009).

Unexplored consequences

However, there are some considerations that escape the analyses of the proponents of the insulation model. First and foremost, in claiming that political concerns should not influence the creation of criminal justice policy they seem not to be concerned with the fact that crime and punishment are societal creations and thus intrinsically connected to the values and choices that people express in political terms (Durkheim 1972). It is impossible to consider crime or punishment thoroughly in 'neutral' or 'non-political' terms – the very notion of crime comes out of political decisions about what to criminalise and to what extent. Even when introducing the classic distinction between *mala prohibita* and *mala in se* one may find shocking examples for what was thought to constitute *mala in se* in different societies and at different times (see, e.g. the exposure of newborns in ancient Greece and Rome or the long lasting non-criminalisation of marital rape.

It is thus inconceivable to eradicate the political element from discussions on crime and punishment, but perhaps that is not what the proponents of the insulation model have in mind. What they are really concerned with is not the political choice involved in crime policy but its abuse in electoral strategies and the heightened public awareness and involvement with its creation (Zimring and Johnson 2006;

Pettit 2002). The issue at hand is therefore not whether political decisions should be made, but by whom and how.

A related issue to ponder at this point is Loader's (2008) notion of 'anti-politics' in the field of criminal justice. In analysing Simon's and Erikson's attempts to depict and explain the current criminal justice transformations (Ericson 2007; Simon 2007), Loader formulates an interesting twist to the politicisation argument, suggesting that perhaps the root of the problem is not the over-politicisation of current criminal justice debates but the very lack of 'politics' in them. What is conducive to more punitive policies is thus the limited manoeuvring field left to politicians at the very tip of culturally acceptable harshness – devoid of any ideological considerations, something that has led to similar policies from either conservative or liberal politicians (cf. e.g. the British New Labour's adoption of the Law & Order dogma).

The propositions to insulate policy-making do not really engage with these questions, but rather choose to cut the Gordian knot by taking criminal justice matters out of the picture altogether. Whether this can be achieved at all will be discussed later. The question at this point is what is left behind and do we really want it? If the *status quo* is so intolerable as to allow for nothing but the shielding of the field, and if the politicians are so cornered by public emotion as to not even be able (or bothered) to pursue their own political values then what we are left with after the isolation of criminal justice policy-making is a very delicate situation. Even if politicians were to pursue such a path, the public would still remain unsatisfied, even more so if the professionals really were to create policies unconcerned with the public sentiment.

The public sentiment is in fact somewhat demonised in the accounts of many of the discussed authors. Zimring and Johnson seem to believe that hostility and antipathy towards offenders are the 'chronic condition in advanced democracies' (2006, 272), while Pettit (2002) believes that responding to public outrage (which in his case at least is not chronic but occasional and instilled by recently exposed 'evils') will unquestionably lead to the maximum levels of harshness. These accounts seem to forget that until the fall of the rehabilitative ideal in the 1970s, the public was rather content with the existing levels of punishment or at least was not actively engaged in seeking for more punitive measures (Loader 2009). The 'outrage spiral', the preconditions for which existed for decades, has only started about thirty or forty years ago and even then only in certain political systems and not everywhere where its necessary conditions were present.

The public opinion is not nearly as clear-cut as some proponents of insulation portray it. Some are more aware of this than others. Lacey (2007), for example points at the intense complexity of the notion and warns against the ease with which it can be manipulated. She uses the argument to emphasise why policy-making should be removed from the public, but her contentions also put in question Zimring and Johnson's (2006) notion of the 'normality of hostility towards offenders'. As Loader

(2008, 10) properly points out, there have been '*moments and places of penal moderation*', that contradict such 'normality' and about which too little is known. Moreover, it seems that the notions of 'redemption' and life changes are at least at times just as powerful as those of revenge and punishment (Maruna 2009).

In this spirit, it is not completely unconceivable for Pettit's outrage spiral to produce outcomes that insulation proponents themselves might favour. For example, in the case of juvenile boot camps in Florida, the death of a young person in such an institution (the exposure of an evil) triggered a major debate (public outrage) and subsequent policy initiatives (reaction), which led to moderate changes in policy and considerable changes in practice (all but one boot camps were eventually closed as a result) (Ciftci et al. 2006).

Public opinion is in fact far from straightforward and cannot simply be deemed punitive (Roberts and Hough 2005). Furthermore, the role of the media in creating the impression of punitiveness needs to be further explored.

Nevertheless, regardless of whether we believe it to be fixed on harshness or not, the problem with disregarding public emotion, is that it 'risks fuelling public resentment and leaving it ripe for demagogic and authoritarian exploitation' (Loader 2009, 10).Widening the gap between the makings of criminal justice and the public could produce further dissatisfaction with the criminal justice system, which could in turn lead to unwanted consequences such as recoiling to private security and ghettoisation (see also Simon 2007) or even acts of violence and vigilantism (Evans 2003).

A further concern in the debate about insulation should be its purpose and motivation. What is it exactly that we want to achieve by shielding criminal policy from the public? It seems apparent that what the proponents have in mind is a more lenient, systematic and efficient criminal justice system than what they face today (Sherman 2009; Zimring and Johnson 2006; Pettit 2002). We have already established that the criteria to measure these features are far from clear, so the results might not be easily determined. For instance, is the imprisonment rate really a good measure of punitiveness? Furthermore, the ideal of having a more moderate system of punishment is not widely shared outside the criminological community. Going back to the argument about disregarding public sentiment, it is necessary to consider whether it is really desirable to design a policy that the majority of the public strongly disagrees with. As painful as it is for a liberally minded criminologist to think about today's levels of harshness in punishment as just and appropriate, if they reflect the level of censure that our society wishes to instil on offenders – shouldn't they perhaps first strive to change (Roberts and Hough 2005) or channel (Loader 2009) the public attitude before changing the policy?

Lastly, a further question raised by the insulation proposition is the unreserved trust that its proponents put in the professional bodies they envision creating criminal justice. While it is readily understandable how the policies produced would be more systematic (Pettit 2002) and perhaps even more evidence based (Sherman 2009), the question about leniency cannot be so easily answered. To believe that professionals in any given field can be entirely neutral might perhaps be conceivable when dealing with hard sciences, but in social sciences it seems rather naive. As discussed earlier, crime is a social construct and in its roots inescapably political – therefore, it cannot be discussed, analysed or even approached in a neutral manner. Professionals too are members of the society and come to the field with very different ideas. There are advocates of leniency among them, but there are also advocates of harsh justice and it is not clear at all that putting professionals in charge would produce radically different outcomes. Seeking reassurance in existing lenient systems with professionalised policy-making (e.g. Tonry 2004) may also be fruitless, as those professionals stem from a different background and it is largely unclear which feature exactly it is that 'produces' leniency.

Conclusion

The questions of criminal justice policy-making are very delicate matters, since it is a field charged with emotions, principles and individual beliefs. Answering the question whether insulating processes of creating such policies is desirable is equally difficult.

On the one hand the desire to curb the mounting harshness in criminal justice, which proponents of the insulation model all display, seems an appropriate and necessary aim. The levels of punitiveness that some systems have reached may properly be deemed immoral on the principled side and economically unsustainable on the more pragmatic one.

On the other hand the means that those authors have chosen to reach that aim – the shielding of policy-making from the 'hostile' public – appears to open more questions than it answers. In many ways this is a step back in history, to a system of 'Platonic guardians' (Loader 2006) that existed before the fall of the rehabilitative ideal and that has been replaced due to reasons we do not yet entirely comprehend. Re-insulating criminal justice may or may not be an unattainable in modern society,[1] but what I find more perturbing about it is the idea in the background of such a proposition.

1 The political feasibility of shielding criminal justice is an issue that authors engage with repeatedly, but a full analysis would exceed the remit of this article. For the most part they see it as a rather achievable aim, mainly claiming that the status quo in criminal justice gives no option for political (electoral) gain to either of the political opponents, thus making 'insulation' an 'opt-out' solution (Lacey 2007; Simon 2007; Pettit 2002). It is highly disputable, however, whether the political reality could indeed produce a 'truce' between parties in order to remove the field from their political and electoral agenda.

Zimring and Johnson, Pettit and others seem to be sure of the fact that public and political presence in criminal justice necessarily implies harshness. They seem to have resigned on the notion of reaching an acceptable system where public sentiment is not ignored, but mitigated and perhaps educated (e.g. Roberts and Hough 2005). Such a position is dangerously pessimistic and 'too readily accepts that what politics has become is all that it can ever be' (Loader 2008, 408), thus allowing us to dismiss thinking about and working for a different kind of politics. In criminal justice, a field historically marked by slow yet undeniable progress towards more and more humane measures, such a position is all the less appealing.

References

Albrecht, Hans-Jörg. 2001. Post-Adjudication Dispositions in Comparative Perspective. In *Sentencing and Sanctions in Western Countries,* edited by M. H. Tonry and R. S. Frase, 293–330. Oxford: Oxford University Press.

Cavadino, Michael, and Dignan, James. 2006. *Penal Systems: A Comparative Approach.* London: Sage.

Ciftci, Sabri, Pesta, George, Oakley, Catherine, and Blomberg, Tom. 2006. Policy-making as Sequential: A Model and Test, Draft paper. [http://works.bepress.com/sabri_ciftci/2, accessed March 7, 2012].

Durkheim, Emile. 1972. *Selected Writings.* Edited by A. Giddens. Cambridge: Cambridge University Press.

Ericson, Richard V. 2007. *Crime in an Insecure World.* Cambridge: Polity.

Evans, Jessica. 2003. Vigilance and Vigilantes: Thinking Psychoanalytically about Anti-paedophile Action. *Theoretical Criminology* 7.2: 163–189.

Fischer, Justina A. V. 2005. The Impact of Direct Democracy on Crime: Is the Median Voter Boundedly Rational? *University of St. Gallen Discussion Paper No. 2005-14.* [http://papers.ssrn.com/sol3/papers.cfm?abstract_id=778984, accessed March 7, 2012].

Garland, David. 2001. *The Culture of Control: Crime and Social Order in Contemporary Society.* Oxford: Oxford University Press.

Lacey, Nicola. 2007. *The Prisoners' Dilemma: Political Economy and Punishment in Contemporary Democracies.* Cambridge: Cambridge University Press.

Loader, Ian. 2006. Fall of the 'Platonic Guardians': Liberalism, Criminology and Political Responses to Crime in England and Wales. *British Journal of Criminology* 46.4: 561–586.

Loader, Ian. 2009. Playing with Fire? Democracy and the Emotions of Crime and Punishment. In *Emotions, Crime and Justice,* edited by S. Karstedt, I. Loader, and H. Strang, 347–362. Oxford: Hart.

Loader, Ian. 2008. The Anti-Politics of Crime. *Theoretical Criminology* 12: 399–410.

Loader, Ian, and Sparks, Richard. 2010. *Public Criminology? Criminological Politics in the Twenty-first Century*. London: Routledge.

Maruna, Shadd. 2009. Redeeming Redemption as a Criminological Concept. In *IX. Conference of the European Society of Criminology*. Ljubljana [http://videolectures.net/esc09_maruna_rrc/ [Accessed December 7, 2011].

Montesquieu, Charles de Secondat. 1989. *The Spirit of the Laws*. Edited by A. M. Cohler, B. C. Miller, and H. S. Stone. Cambridge: Cambridge University Press.

Nelken, David. 2009. Comparative Criminal Justice: Beyond Ethnocentrism and Relativism. *European Journal of Criminology* 6.4: 291–311.

Nelken, David. 2006. Patterns of Punitiveness. *Modern Law Review* 69.2: 262–277.

Pettit, Philip N. 2002. Is Criminal Justice Politically Feasible? *Buffalo Criminal Law Review* 5: 427–450.

Rawls, John. 1993. *Political Liberalism*. New York: Columbia University Press.

Roberts, Julian V., and Hough, Mike J. 2005. *Understanding Public Attitudes to Criminal Justice*. Buckingham: Open University Press.

Sherman, Lawrence W. 2009. Evidence and liberty: The Promise of Experimental Criminology. *Journal of Criminology and Criminal Justice* 9.1: 5–28.

Simon, Jonathan. 2007. *Governing Through Crime: How the War on Crime Transformed American Democracy and Created a Culture of Fear*. Oxford: Oxford University Press.

Tham, Henrik. 2001. Law and Order as a Leftist Project?: The Case of Sweden. *Punishment Society* 3.3: 409–426.

Tocqueville, Alexis de. 2003. *Democracy in America*. Edited by B. Frohnen. Washington: Regnery Gateway.

Tonry, Michael. 2007. Determinants of Penal Policies. In *Crime, Punishment and Politics in Comparative Perspective*, edited by Michael Tonry, 1–48. Chicago: University Of Chicago Press.

Tonry, Michael. 2004. Why aren't German Penal Policies Harsher and Imprisonment Rates Higher? *German Law Journal* 5.10.

Wacquant, Loïc. 2009. *Punishing the Poor: The Neoliberal Government of Social Insecurity*. Durham (ND): Duke University Press.

Whitman, James Q. 2005. *Harsh justice*. Oxford: Oxford University Press.

Zimring, Franklin E. and Johnson, David T. 2006. Public Opinion and the Governance of Punishment in Democratic Political Systems. *The Annals of the American Academy of Political and Social Science* 605.1: 265–280.

Zimring, Franklin E., Hawkins, Gordon, and Kamin, Sam. 2003. *Punishment and Democracy*. Oxford: Oxford University Press.

Introduction of Criminal Law Powers in Other Legal Procedures: A Convenient Bypass for Obtaining Evidence?

Sabina Zgaga

Introduction

In Slovenian law, several new types of non-criminal legal procedure against criminal conduct have been introduced recently. This paper analyses the powers Slovenian Police can exert in the procedure provided for by the State Border Control Act (SBCA). These powers are rather similar to those of the criminal procedure. Similar rules apply also to Slovenian Customs under the Custom Service Act (CSA). Conditions for the exercise of these investigative powers in border and customs procedures are less strict and can enable the police to bypass the stricter regulation of the Criminal Procedure Act (CPA). The main focus of this paper is on the question whether such powers and their regulation is contentious from the viewpoint of the Constitution of Slovenia, if such an extension of criminal law powers weakens human rights protection, and whether evidence, obtained according to SBCA or CSA can be used in criminal procedure.

The first part of this paper discusses the powers of the Slovenian police granted by these *leges speciales*. The second part focuses on the constitutional regulation of relevant human rights (protection of dwellings and the right to privacy and personality rights) and the potential issues that arise from the constitutional viewpoint in Slovenia or some other jurisdictions (USA and the European Court for Human Rights). The third part compares these regulations with their counterparts laid down in the CPA, and offers an answer to the question as to whether and under which conditions evidence obtained according to SBCA or CSA can be used in criminal procedure.

Border powers

Under SBCA, police officers may perform checks on persons, vehicles, and goods (Art. 29 SBCA). Police officers may also examine and search persons in the event of a suspicion of possession of prohibited items, objects, or to establish the identity of persons. Examinations may cover everything but for the examination of body cavities (ibid.). If we consider the nature of the human rights that are limited (privacy and personality rights, Art. 35 of Slovenian Constitution) and the degree of its limitation, this act of investigation qualitatively equals to personal search under CPA (Art. 214–219 CPA).

Police officers may also examine vehicles with the aim of preventing illegal entry to Slovenia or in case there is suspicion that a person within the vehicle is transporting prohibited objects or items that would help to establish the identity of the same person or other passengers. This means a detailed inspection of all parts of the vehicle, including the dismantling of its individual parts (Art. 29 SBCAct).[1] It seems that vehicle examination under SBCA with its detailed inspection comprises the search of concealed spaces in the vehicle. For such examinations in criminal procedure, the provisions of house search should apply, and according to the CPA 'the provisions referring to house and personal searches shall also apply *mutatis mutandis* to searches of concealed spaces in means of transport' (Art. 215, para. 6 CPA).

The inviolability of dwellings and privacy and personality rights in the Constitution of Slovenia

Regarding the nature and degree of the mentioned powers the following constitutional rights are relevant: the right to privacy and personality rights (Art. 35 of Slovenian Constitution) and the inviolability of dwellings (ibid., art. 36.)

According to Article 36 of the Slovenian Constitution, dwellings are inviolable. The Constitution demands a court order or the consent of the resident for entrance to and search of the dwellings. Any person whose dwelling or other premises are searched has the right to be present or to have a representative present and such search may only be conducted in the presence of two witnesses. However, subject to conditions provided by law, an official may enter the dwelling or other premises of another person without a court order, and may in exceptional circumstances conduct a search in the absence of witnesses, when this is absolutely necessary for the direct apprehension of a person who has committed a criminal offence or in order to protect people or property.

1 For similar powers of custom officials see art. 27 CSA.

The search of vehicles' concealed spaces, which would certainly happen in case of dismantling individual parts of the vehicle according to the State Border Control Act, should certainly fall under this article. Although the Constitutional Court generally decided that a vehicle in traffic does not equal to a dwelling with regard to protection of privacy (Decision of Slovenian Constitutional court, Up-1293/08, para. 24). in my opinion an expectation of privacy should be acknowledged in its concealed spaces, at least to some level (see Gorkič 2011, 9).

This conclusion opens up two possible problems. First, for a house search either a court order or the resident's permission is needed. The State Border Control Act, however, requires neither for the inspection of a vehicle's concealed parts. In this regard, the State Border Control Act could be considered unconstitutional, if the constitutional conditions for entrance and inspection without court order are not fulfilled (most likely the exception of protecting people or property). The Slovenian Constitutional Court in such manner enumerated four reasons for the absence of a court order in case of vehicle inspection performed by a custom officer, due to a lower expectation of privacy in vehicles: the special regulation of road traffic because of its dangerousness; a vehicle usually does not serve as residence or repository of personal effects; the sovereign authority of a nation to regulate who and what comes within its borders to secure its safety, additionally emphasised by Slovenia's accession to the European Union (EU) and its Schengen obligations; finally, the nature of border inspection, which requires it to be performed quickly (Decision of Slovenian Constitutional court, Up-1293/08, paras. 24, 25, and 26).

I agree that these reasons can lower the expectation of privacy but in my view, they do not abolish it completely. These can be valid reasons for not demanding a court order. However, some protection of privacy should still be awarded and a rightful distinction between different levels of invasion of privacy should be made. In this respect especially the constitutional principle of proportionality, which will be discussed later, should be taken into consideration.

According to the Slovenian Constitution, the inviolability of the physical and mental integrity of every person, his privacy and personality rights shall also be guaranteed. This constitutional right is relevant concerning both the personal check and the check of goods. Nevertheless, since this constitutional provision does not include any additional requirements and conditions, only the general conditions for the regulation of constitutional rights should be observed, such as, again, the principle of proportionality.

The Relationship between the State Border Control Act and the Criminal Procedure Act

Although equal investigative powers (personal search and vehicle or house search) can be used according to both acts, the conditions for performing these powers in criminal procedure are much stricter. According to CPA for house search, usually a court order, two witnesses, justified grounds for the suspicion, and other conditions must be fulfilled, while according to the State Border Control Act only grounds for suspicion and a special justification of the performed measure suffice for a very thorough examination of vehicle.

In addition, according to CPA, for personal search again a court order, two witnesses, justified grounds for the suspicion, and other conditions must be fulfilled, while according to State Border Control Act only grounds for suspicion of possession of prohibited items or objects or the aim to establish a person's identity suffice, although the examination includes everything but examination of body cavities.

In my opinion such a relationship between the conditions according to CPA and the State Border Control Act contradicts the constitutional principle of proportionality. According to this principle when investigating graver criminal acts graver infringements of constitutional rights are allowed. The opposite is also true: not every infringement of constitutional rights is allowed when investigating lesser criminal acts or misdemeanours. Yet, currently, it is easier to perform these measures when trying to prevent possession of prohibited items or objects, illegal entry into Slovenia, or just to establish the identity of persons or passengers in a vehicle (i.e. acts which are not always even misdemeanours, let alone criminal acts), than while investigating a criminal act according to CPA. According to the principle of proportionality, it should be the other way around. Powers to perform these investigative measures should be wider in criminal procedure which deals with punishing and preventing criminal acts, than in procedure according to the State Border Control Act, which 'only' tries to prevent acts that are not even always misdemeanours.

A further concern is that such regulations also seem to grant an opportunity for officers to perform such measures according to this act rather than according to CPA and later use the evidence, obtained in this procedure, for criminal prosecution and thereby to bypass the CPA regulation.

There are two potential interpretations of this latter issue. According to the first interpretation, the conditions of the State Border Control Act suffice for the validity of such evidence in criminal procedure. If the investigative measure is performed according to the rules and the evidence is obtained while performing it, the evidence can be used. The State Border Control Act regulates such situations in the following way. When goods are found during the inspection or examination of a person, goods, or vehicle, which may be seized pursuant to the CPA, the officer should follow CPA from this point on (Art. 31 SBCA). This enables the use of evidence in criminal procedure, even though they were obtained according to very low conditions. Only after the potentially incriminatory nature of such evidence is recognised, the higher conditions of CPA apply for the further procedure but not for the evaluation of the validity of evidence.

According to the second and stricter interpretation, evidence cannot be used in criminal procedure, since the stricter conditions of criminal procedure and constitutional conditions were not applied. The Slovenian Constitutional Court has already decided in a similar matter.[2] A custom officer performed visual check of the petitioner's vehicle at the Slovenian border and noticed a physical alteration of the vehicle. He used a dog, which indicated that there could be drug in the vehicle. After dismantling the vehicle and checking it with the endoscope, the custom officer found a suspicious wrapping (the drug). Police was later notified and they performed a thorough search of the vehicle. The drug was used as evidence in the criminal procedure against the petitioner.

The petitioner claimed that the custom officer's vehicle search had not been performed according to CPA (no court order for inspection) and therefore cannot be used in criminal procedure (Decision of Slovenian Constitutional court Up-1293/08, paras. 20 and 21).

The Slovenian Constitutional Court based its decision on a previous decision according to which a vehicle is usually not a concealed space, where expectation of privacy is reasonable. Partly due to the petitioner's poor argumentation, who did not claim that vehicles should in certain cases be awarded reasonable expectation of privacy, this reasoning prevented the assessment of the constitutionality of vehicle checks against Article 36 (the inviolability of dwellings) (Gorkič 2011, 9). Instead, the court assessed its compliance with Article 35 of the Slovenian Constitution (protection of right to privacy and personality rights) and decided that due to a lesser degree of reasonable expectation of privacy (see above) and the practical inefficiency of inspection if a court order had been needed, a court order was not needed for inspection of vehicles in customs procedure.

To some extent the Slovenian Constitutional Court followed in this decision relevant case law of the US Supreme Court and the European Court for Human Rights (ECHR) but in my opinion it should have decided the case a bit more cautiously. American law does not offer searches at borders the same level of protection under the Fourth Amendment[3] as to other searches – this is due to lower expectation of

2 Decision of Slovenian Constitutional court Up-1293/08 dealt with a procedure according to Custom Service Act, which regulates similar powers and conditions for vehicle search as State Border Control Act.

3 Fourth Amendment of the Constitution of the United States: 'The right of the people to be secure in their persons, houses, papers, and effects, against unreasonable searches and seizures, shall not be

privacy and the State's sovereign authority to regulate who and what comes within its border (Kim 2009, 1). However, there are also restrictions to such searches. Firstly, any search must still be reasonable. This requires balancing the intrusion on the individual's Fourth Amendment interests against the promotion of legitimate governmental interests. The government must justify its intrusion of a legitimate expectation of privacy (ibid., 6).[4] Secondly, there is a distinction between routine and non-routine searches. Routine searches do not demand any ground for suspicion, but represent a lower invasion of privacy (travellers may be stopped at fixed checkpoints near the border without individualised suspicion even if the stop is based largely on ethnicity (US v. Montoya de Hernandez) and exposed to removal, disassembling, and reassembling a vehicle's fuel tank (ibid.) document check, pat-downs, emptying of pockets, etc. (Kim 2009, 1). Non-routine searches (destructive searches of inanimate objects, prolonged detentions, strip searches, body cavity searches, X-ray searches, ibid.) demand reasonable suspicion (US v. Montoya de Hernandez), because they present a graver intrusion of privacy. Reasonable suspicion is less than probable cause,[5] but officials at the border must have a particularised and objective basis for suspecting the particular person of something illegal (US v. Montoya de Hernandez). Thirdly, these powers can only be performed at the border, which is very strictly defined (Kim 2009, 1).

Comparing the Slovenian and the American powers of the border police it can be inferred that both systems differentiate between powers which can be performed without any standard of proof for illicit behaviour, and a second group of powers that can only be performed at a certain higher standard of proof. The powers, divided into these two groups, are not altogether equal. Some powers of the Slovenian police demand higher standard of proof than the similar ones of the American police and *vice versa*. Thirdly, under American law, the more intrusive powers can only be performed at the border, whereas in Slovenia the more intrusive powers can also be performed on the territory of Slovenia as compensatory measures (Art. 35–36 SBCA). Fourthly, the American standard of reasonable suspicion is stricter than the Slovenian grounds for suspicion which is the lowest possible standard of proof in Slovenian (criminal) legislation. Reasonable suspicion must have a particularised and objective basis for suspecting the particular person of something illegal, whereas grounds for suspicion do not demand that they are directed towards a known person and can be based on any minimal notification (Decision of Slovenian Constitutional Court, U-I-25/95, para. 53), even by an anonymous person.

violated, and no Warrants shall issue, but upon probable cause, supported by Oath or affirmation, and particularly describing the place to be searched, and the persons or things to be seized.'

4 See also United States v. Montoya de Hernandez, and United States v. Manuel Flores-Montano

5 This standard of proof is usually required for a Fourth Amendment search.

The ECHR has dealt with criminal law powers from non-criminal procedures in very few cases from the viewpoint of the right to privacy and family life,[6] because these cases have been mainly dealt with from the viewpoint of the right to the peaceful enjoyment of possessions[7] (alleged wrongful seizure of the possession).[8] From its case law, it can be inferred that the ECHR does not generally contradict the use of criminal law powers in non-criminal procedures. In case *Funke v. France*, where custom officials with the help of police performed a house search and seized some evidence according to the existing legislation, the court stated that

> undoubtedly, in the field under consideration (the prevention of capital outflows and tax evasion) the states encounter serious difficulties [...]. The court therefore recognises that they may consider it necessary to have recourse to measures such as house searches and seizures in order to obtain physical evidence of exchange control offences and, where appropriate, to prosecute those responsible. (Funke v. France, para. 56.)

However, 'the relevant legislation and practice must afford adequate and effective safeguards against abuse' (ibid.). Following this, the ECHR reached a conclusion that there was a breach of protection of privacy and family life, since 'the customs authorities had *very wide powers*; in particular, they had *exclusive competence to assess the expediency, number, length and scale of inspections*. Above all, in the absence of any requirement of a judicial warrant the *restrictions and conditions provided for in law*, which were emphasised by the Government,[9] *appear too lax and full of loopholes* for the interferences with the applicant's rights to have been strictly proportionate to the legitimate aim pursued' (ibid., para. 57).

Applying this decision to Slovenian regulation, one might assess that powers of the Slovenian police officials are as wide as were the ones of the French custom officials, since they can decide themselves, which power they will execute and they can

6 Art. 8 of European Convention for Protection of Human Rights: 'Everyone has the right to respect for his private and family life, his home and his correspondence. There shall be no interference by a public authority with the exercise of this right except such as is in accordance with the law and is necessary in a democratic society in the interests of national security, public safety or the economic well-being of the country, for the prevention of disorder or crime, for the protection of health or morals, or for the protection of the rights and freedoms of others.'

7 Art. 1 of Protocol 1 to the European Convention for Protection of Human Rights.

8 See cases C. M. v. France, Butler v. United Kingdom and Ismayilov v. Russia.

9 Funke v. France, para. 54: 'Such persons, however, had the benefit of substantial safeguards, strengthened by very rigorous judicial supervision: decision-making by the head of the customs district concerned, the rank of the officers authorised to establish offences, the presence of a senior police officer (officier de police judiciaire), the timing of searches, the preservation of lawyers' and doctors' professional secrecy, the possibility of invoking the liability of the public authorities, etc. In short, even before the reform of 1986–89, the French system had ensured that there was a proper balance between the requirements of law enforcement and the protection of the rights of the individual.'

search and inspect anything and anyone (unless body cavities), based on grounds of suspicion only. According to the State Border Control Act, there is no special judicial supervision, except for judicial review of administrative acts according to Article 157 of the Slovenian Constitution.

There have also been other relevant decisions by the ECHR. In the case *Gillan and Quinton v. United Kingdom* the ECHR repeated the statement from *Foka v. Turkey*, where the applicant was subjected to a forced search of her bag by border guards that 'any search effected by the authorities on a person interferes with his or her private life' (Gillan and Quinton v. UK, para. 61). Therefore, privacy is awarded protection and any intrusion must be made in accordance with law and necessary in modern society for achieving certain ECHR aims. In *Gillan and Quinton v. UK* the court dealt with a detailed search of the petitioner's person for anti-terrorism campaign, which could be performed at random, without any grounds. The individual could be stopped anywhere and at any time, without notice and without any choice as to whether or not to submit to a search. The court considered that 'the powers of authorisation and confirmation as well as those of stop and search were neither sufficiently circumscribed nor subject to adequate legal safeguards against abuse, therefore were not in accordance with the law' (ibid., para. 87). This argumentation could apply also to complementary measures according to the State Border Control Act, which can be performed everywhere inside Slovenia.

However, the court has already narrowed down the scope of its reasoning, since it stated that on contrary, it does not apply to airport checks (and therefore probably neither to other border checks), since 'an air traveller may be seen as consenting to such a search by choosing to travel. He knows that he and his bags are liable to be searched before boarding the aeroplane and has a freedom of choice, since he can leave personal items behind and walk away without being subjected to a search' (ibid., para. 64). The key issue here is the consent of the traveller; however, this should be also balanced with the right to free movement.

Following the analysis of decisions by the Slovenian Constitutional Court, the American Supreme Court and ECHR, I must unfortunately summon up that all three approve of lower standards for border powers in comparison to the same powers in criminal procedure. However, it still strikes me as strange that the Slovenian Constitutional Court declared that some powers in criminal procedure can only be used for the investigation of the gravest criminal acts. However, it did not apply the same principle to the relation between criminal procedure and border control procedure.

Due to the special nature of procedures according to the State Border Control Act (quick procedures, crowd of people, etc.), there should surely be some specialities to enable a more swift and expedient procedure. This could eliminate the court order even for more intense invasions of privacy. However, I still believe that the standard of proof for these more intense powers should be higher than mere grounds for suspicion, which can be completely subjective. The standard should be in some way objectified, as the reasonable suspicion in USA is.

Concerning the use of evidence from non-criminal procedure in criminal procedure, I agree that there cannot be a general prohibition of using such evidence in criminal procedure. However, there is a danger that officers would rather use investigative measures according to non-criminal procedures, because their conditions for equal investigative measures are less strict. For example, if a police officer does not have grounds for a search of concealed parts of a vehicle, he would call in a colleague from customs to perform the same measure according to custom regulations and later use the evidence in a criminal procedure.

In my opinion, a compromise between both extreme interpretations should be reached: the plain view doctrine. Note that this situation is similar to the situation when the police are performing a house search for a certain criminal act and find evidence for another criminal act. Evidence, obtained according to the State Border Control Act should therefore be allowed to be used also in criminal procedure, if the additional conditions of the plain view doctrine are rationally fulfilled. These conditions are (Zupančič et al. 2001, 565):

- prior justification: the officer performing the powers is legally on the premises. In our case this means that all conditions of the measure according to the special legislation are fulfilled;
- immediately apparent incriminating nature of the evidence;
- lawful right to access the evidence;
- there is no case of timed arrests. In our case this means that the measure was not performed deliberately at such time and place which would give the officer the power to perform an investigating measure and obtain the evidence;
- inadvertence of the evidence. In my opinion this condition is crucial, since it prevents abuses of the less strict non-criminal legislation.

Conclusion

My argument leads to the following conclusions. Firstly, a clear distinction should be made between less and more intrusive powers. Due to the special nature of procedures according to the State Border Control Act, some specificities should be made for both groups of measures in order to enable a more swift and expedient procedure. However, the standard of proof for the more intense powers should be higher than the grounds for suspicion. It should be objectified, as is the reasonable suspicion in USA.

These issues have raised numerous constitutional questions that have not been addressed or answered completely. Due to the current trends of efficiency, the initial thesis must unfortunately be confirmed. The spread of criminal law powers into other procedures does not mean also the spread of constitutional safeguards. To the contrary, it is easier to perform equal powers in non-criminal procedures than in criminal procedure, even though in non-criminal procedures only misdemeanours or just financial interests of the state are at stake. Consequently, non-criminal procedures are easily abused for obtaining evidence for criminal prosecution.

Concerning the powers of police officers according to the State Border Control Act, a compromise should be reached between both extreme interpretations (prohibition or simple permission of the use of evidence in criminal procedures) in form of the plain view doctrine. Evidence, obtained in a procedure according to the State Border Control Act, should therefore be allowed to be used in criminal procedure, if the additional conditions of the plain view doctrine are fulfilled, with special regard to the evidence's inadvertence.

References

Gorkič, Primož. 2011. Dokazi, pridobljeni pri carinskem nadzoru ob prehodu državne meje v kazenskem postopku. [Use of evidence, resulting from the custom's border control, in criminal procedure.] *Pravna praksa* 31: 9–12.

Kim, Yule. 2009. Protecting the U.S. Perimeter: Border Searcher under the Fourth Amendment. Washington: Congressional Research Service.

Zupančič, Boštjan. ed. 2001. *Ustavno kazensko procesno pravo. [Constitutional criminal procedural law.]* Ljubljana: Pasadena.

Legislation

Constitution of the Republic of Slovenia, Unofficial Consolidated Text [http://www.us-rs.si/en/about-the-court/legal-basis/constitution/, accessed on 16.12. 2011].

Criminal Procedure Act, Unofficial Consolidated Text [http://www.dz-rs.si/index.php?id=101&vt=1&cl=K&mandate=-1&unid=UPB|E9AF40467BDF77D9C125770A00243BD7&showdoc=1, accessed on 16.12.2011].

Custom Service Act, Unofficial Consolidated text [http://www.dz-rs.si/wps/portal/Home/deloDZ/zakonodaja/izbranZakonAkt?uid=C08D7E81CFC097D1C1257847002C5EC9&db=urad_prec_bes&mandat=VI, accessed on 10.4.2012].

Prevention of the Restriction of Competition Act, Unofficial Consolidated Text [http://www.dz-rs.si/wps/portal/Home/deloDZ/zakonodaja/izbranZakonAkt?uid=6393F2FC7C1ED219C12579440023048E&db=urad_prec_bes&mandat=V, accessed on 24.12.2011].

State Border Control Act, Official consolidated text (ZNDM-2-UPB1), http://www.policija.si/eng/images/stories/Legislation/pdf/StateBorderControlAct2010.pdf, accessed on 20.3.2012].

Cases

Slovenia

U-I-25/95, Constitutional Court of Republic of Slovenia, 27th November 1997.

Up 430/00, Constitutional Court of Republic of Slovenia, 10th October 2002.

Up 1293/08, Constitutional Court of Republic of Slovenia, 6th July 2011.

United States

Montoya de Hernandez, 473 U.S. 531 (1985).

United States v. Manuel Flores-Montano, 541 U.S. 149 (2004).

European Court of Human Rights

Foka v. Turkey, 28940/95, 24th June 2008.

Funke v. France, 10828/84, 25th February 1995.

Gillan and Quinton v. United Kingdom, 4158/05, 12th January 2010.

Central and Eastern European Forum for Legal, Political, and Social Theory Yearbook

Edited by Jürgen Busch / Péter Cserne / Michael Hein / Miklós Könczöl / Miodrag Jovanović / Marta Soniewicka

Vol. 1 Péter Cserne / Miklós Könczöl (eds.): Legal and Political Theory in the Post-National Age. Selected papers presented at the Second Central and Eastern European Forum for Legal, Political and Social Theorists (Budapest, 21–22 May 2010). 2011.

Vol. 2 Miodrag A. Jovanović / Bojan Spaić (eds.): Jurisprudence and Political Philosophy in the 21st Century. Reassessing Legacies. 2012.

Vol. 3 Péter Cserne / Miklós Könczöl / Marta Soniewicka (eds.): The Rule of Law and the Challenges to Jurisprudence. Selected papers presented at the Fourth Central and Eastern European Forum for Legal, Political and Social Theorists, Celje, 23–24 March 2012. 2014.

www.peterlang.com

www.ingramcontent.com/pod-product-compliance
Ingram Content Group UK Ltd.
Pitfield, Milton Keynes, MK11 3LW, UK
UKHW021842100926
8556IPUK00019B/992

9 783631 643815